BLACK SQUARE & COMPASS
200 YEARS OF PRINCE HALL FREEMASONRY

JOSEPH A. WALKES, JR., P.M., 33⁰
Mr. Walkes has also written The Documentary History of King Solomon Lodge No. 15, F. & A.M. He's a Fellow and President of the Phylaxis Society and owns the Walkes Prince Hall Masonic Collection thought to be the world's largest privately owned collection on Prince Hall Masonry.

Black Square & Compass

200 Years of Prince Hall Freemasonry

Joseph A. Walkes, Jr.

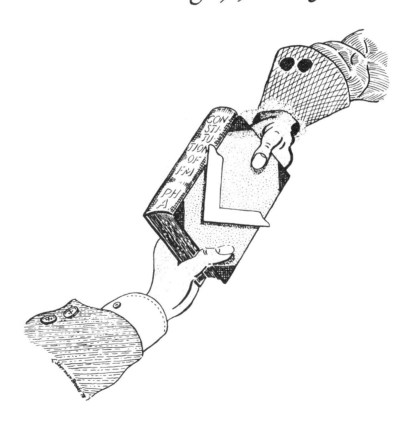

Macoy Publishing & Masonic Supply Co., Inc.
Richmond, Virginia 23228

Second Printing	October, 1979
Third Printing	June, 1980
Revised Edition	1981
Fourth Printing	1989
Fifth Printing	1994
Sixth Printing	2006

by Macoy Publishing & Masonic Supply Co., Inc.
Richmond, Virginia 23228

ISBN-0-88053-061-8

L.C. Catalog Card No. 79-112352

Printed in the United States of America

DEDICATION

To DR. JOHN G. LEWIS, JR.

Sovereign Grand Commander, United Supreme Council, 33° Ancient and Accepted Scottish Rite of Freemasonry, Prince Hall Affiliation, Southern Jurisdiction, United States of America, and

To DR. CHARLES H. WESLEY

Author of *Prince Hall: Life and Legacy*

"It has been customary for Masonry to perform her deeds without the blare of bugle or the sound of trumpet. It has been traditional that such acts of which I speak tonight go unnoticed and unsung. Just the other day in the office of the Executive Director of our Conference, (of Prince Hall Grand Masters) Most Worshipful Amos T. Hall, I noticed the series of books lately published giving the story of the Negro in America. At no point did I find a chronicle of the work and influence of the Masonic institution or the part it played in giving a struggling race direction as it trudged laboriously up freedom's road. Many of Masonry's illustrious sons were mentioned but no mention or thought given to the institution that sustained them and bore them safely over their periods of depression and frustration. If this night brings an end to that, then so mote it be!"

JNO G. LEWIS, JR.

Statement of the occasion at the Testimonial Dinner for the Honorable Thurgood Marshall 33°, 1966.

FOREWORD

I have been quite elated over the reception of the first edition of my book. The first edition was printed in a limited supply, and was exhausted in a short period.

For the most part, the "feed-back" received from those that read the book were quite positive. The one noticeable exception being from a well known Masonic book reviewer, whose reviews are carried in a number of Caucasian Masonic publications. After reading my book, he refused to review it, and I was informed that he found the work to be militant! Here again is another case of the abuse that Prince Hall Freemasonry endures at the hands of its counterparts. Why is it that a Black man writes or says something and a Caucasian takes exceptions to it, and without saying why, declares it as "militant"? I wonder what right has a so-called Masonic book reviewer to decide, merely because he does not like a work, to ignore it. Such people do more harm to the Masonic fraternity than those who would burn books.

Another criticism received was from a retired Lieutenant Colonel from Texas, a Caucasian Freemason who accused me of preaching a "Black-power" Masonry.

To such criticism, I must answer that my book was written to present some of the *Masonic roots of Prince Hall Freemasonry* and the history of those who represent the "power and glory" of our fraternity. If that be militant and black power, then, so be it. But only a fool would use such words! Masonic history cannot be defined in those terms.

One area not covered and deliberately left out is the argument over the *regularity* of Prince Hall Freemasonry. This debate has been raging for 200 years, and is senseless. PRINCE HALL FREEMASONRY IS A REALITY, IT HAS BEEN A REALITY FOR 200 YEARS, AND IT SHALL REMAIN A REALITY AS LONG AS FREEMASONRY EXISTS IN THE UNITED STATES OF AMERICA.

Those who call it irregular," or "clandestine," or "non-Masonic" are either blind or fools or worse, racist. When one compares the descent and doctrine of Prince Hall Freemasonry with its Caucasian counterparts, one will find very little difference.

Throughout my book, I have leveled criticism at those who continue to stick their heads in the sands, and those who think they can write about the Black experience in America, without knowledge of that Black experience.

> "...given the multicultural nature of American society, we must be extremely cautious in interpreting the experiences of Black people in this country...American society encompasses a variety of systems of cultural definition, some of which are fundamentally different in nature. Within this sociocultural context one must be cautious not to use the framework of experiences of one racial-cultural group to interpret and explain the experience of another."
>
> JOSEPH A. BALDWIN
> "The Journal of Black Psychology"
> *February, 1979, Vol. 5*

Finally, this book was dedicated to two Prince Hall Freemasons whom I held in the highest regards, as men and Masons. At the time of the final publication of *Black Square & Compass*, death claimed the life of perhaps the greatest Prince Hall Freemason who has ever lived. Dr. John G. Lewis, Jr., Grand Master of the Prince Hall Grand Lodge of Louisiana and Sovereign Grand Commander of the United Supreme Council, 33⁰, A.A.S.R., Southern Jurisdiction, a dear and close friend of mine. It was Dr. Lewis, more than any other individual, who motivated me to this love which I carry for Masonry. It is a love that I am proud of.

JOSEPH A. WALKES, JR.

Leavenworth, Kansas—July, 1979

PREFACE BY THE PUBLISHER

In 1903 the Macoy Publishing & Masonic Supply Company published Grimshaw's *Official History of Freemasonry among the Colored People in North America*. Unfortunately, this work proved in ensuing years to be erroneous in many respects, Mr. Grimshaw having embroidered many of his facts with wishful thinking. Unfortunate, too, that many writers have continued to give credence to the Grimshaw book which has caused misleading foundations of thought for their promulgated theses.

And so, it is with no little feeling of gratitude that the same publishing firm has this opportunity, 78 years later, to publish another book authored by a Black Freemason which we hope will serve to rectify past conceptions and beliefs. While some—both Black and White—may not agree with all of Mr. Walkes' presentation in this present work, it must be recognized that Mr. Walkes has "done his homework" and has spent years of research before arriving at and presenting his views. He has referenced his work well and gives many verbatim writings, as well as reproductions of letters, papers, certificates, etc. to write his story from a Black Freemason's viewpoint. This is as it should be and we agree with the author who states that it has been necessary that a Black man give us these facts as no White author could approach the subject with the same feeling. That is not to say that there have not been White Freemasons who have espoused the Black Freemason's cause.

Certainly, early records and minutes were often lost or not recorded at all and the "legitimacy" in the formation of lodges in many instances is clouded—both among the Black and White Masonic lodges. Since the REAL purpose of Freemasonry is to make good men better, then certainly we should be done with nit-picking about the Prince Hall Masonic Fraternity who have contributed a great deal to the betterment and education of their people and this nation in their two centuries of work. Their continued striving for education has shown remarkable progress; their youth movement with forward looking programs for the future generations is enviable.

It is with pleasure that we can offer this book. While we may not agree with all of Mr. Walkes' conclusions or arguments, if we wish to approach the entire subject with an open mind, we will be the richer for reading how and why and what the Black Freemason thinks. And this is the beginning for a better understanding among all mankind.

THE PUBLISHER

1981

CONTENTS

ILLUSTRATIONS

INTRODUCTION

I was made a Prince Hall Master Mason in Cecil A. Ellis, Sr. Lodge No. 110 in Karlsruhe, Germany while a member of the U.S. Army in 1965.

This Lodge, which in short order, I became Master of and eventually wrote a brief history of, was a military Lodge chartered by the P.H. Grand Lodge of Maryland.

Like most newly raised Master Masons my interest to discover and to learn everything, and my enthusiasm for the Craft was boundless.

As, has always been a part of my make-up, I sought answers of my newly discovered fraternity through books. And it was through them that I soon began to learn what must be described as the beauty of Freemasonry, which in turn opened a new world for my inquisitive mind to explore.

But I was soon to discover that there was nothing readily available concerning the Prince Hall fraternity.

My first encounter of the subject was articles written by Caucasian "regular" Freemasons. Some of these "Masonic scholars," I had come to respect for their knowledge in other areas of Freemasonry, were for the most part critical if not down right hostile towards Prince Hall and the fraternity that he had founded.

It was truly a bitter disappointment to me, a bitter pill which forged a determination to discard what I felt to be the white man's basis in reason, which he had devised for the rejection of the Black man and his Masonry. It was also a determination to seek the truth of the matter outside of the culture of racism which I felt was Caucasian American Freemasonry.

What I had to learn was that without understanding the historical context of this ideology of Masonic racism, the Prince Hall Freemason can easily become swallowed up in self doubt and uncertainty, truly wondering if his Masonry was indeed Freemasonry.

As I can remember, one of my first introductions to the subject of the Black man and his Masonry was the writings of Albert Mackey, who was opposed to Masonry for the Black man. What was to be learned later was the fact that during the Civil War, Mackey had to go before Black Union Troops and plead with them to save his city and later witness these Black soldiers march through and occupy his home town of Charleston, S.C. This fact would not be discovered in Masonic books, but only in the works that detailed the Black experience in America. With these Black troops there was also a Prince Hall military Lodge attached.

With detailed research and study of the Black experience, together with the history of Prince Hall Freemasonry, a number of areas can be placed into their proper perspective. Yet, the simple undeniable fact is often overlooked. That is, that Prince Hall Freemasonry is an actuality and will remain so. The fact that organized Caucasian Freemasonry does not accept it, and have attacked the Black man and his Masonry for 200 years, will always leave them open to the charge of racism; a charge that there is no defense against; a charge that very well may eventually destroy the American system of Masonry as we know it, and to the shame of the entire Masonic community other than the Prince Hall fraternity which is the true Brotherhood.

"Let not the 12 (now 30) million Negroes be ashamed of the fact that they are the grandchildren of slaves," said Mahatma Gandhi in 1929. "There is no dishonor in being slaves. There is dishonor in being slave owners."

But let us not think of dishonor in connection with the past. Let us realize that the future is with those who would be truthful, pure and loving. For, as the old wise men have said, "truth ever is, untruth never was. Love alone binds and truth and love occur only to the truly humble."

To place the history of Caucasian Freemasonry and its relationships with the Black man and his Freemasonry, in their proper perspectives, one merely needs to view the proceedings of the two bodies on the same subject, compare it with events recorded in the Black experience outside of the fraternal order, and present the facts.

"...somebody in each era must make clear the facts with utter disregard to his own wish and desire and belief," wrote the Black scholar/historian W.E.B. Du Bois, a Prince Hall Freemason. "What we have got to know, so far as possible, are the things that actually happened in the world...the historian has no right, posing as scientist, to conceal or distort facts, and until we distinguish between these two functions of the chronicles of human action, we are going to render it easy for a muddled world out of sheer ignorance to make the same mistake ten times over." (*Black Reconstruction*, p. 722)

The two most interesting works on Prince Hall Freemasonry were Harry E. Davis' *History of Freemasonry Among The Negro in the United States* and Harold Van Buren Voorhis' *Negro Freemasonry in the United States*. These two works with their wealth of material were the catalyst that inspired me into the pursuit of Masonic research, which has over the years given me so much pleasure. The history by Davis, a Prince Hall Freemason, is by far one of the best written on the subject. There are some errors but such take little from the work.

While on the other hand, Voorhis, who continued his investigation into the history of Prince Hall Freemasonry realized that his book contained glaring errors and therefore withdrew his book from the market.

Voorhis, a Caucasian Freemason, supports my contention that; (1) the history of the Black man in America is the history of Prince Hall Freemasonry and that; (2) the history of Prince Hall Freemasonry must be written by the Black Prince Hall Freemason, for only he can understand and interpret the Black experience.

I have attempted to prove this in the articles I have published over the years in the Phylaxis Magazine, which today stands as the most unique publication in Prince Hall Freemasonry. The history of this Society is presented in this work.

To put together any work, credit must be given to a number of people, without whose interest and assistance, none of this would be accomplished. Listing all would consume more space than I have, but there are a few who must be mentioned. Mrs. Mary Jo Nelson, Librarian, Command and General Staff College, Fort Leavenworth, Kansas. It was this young lady who put up with my seemingly unsatiable thirst to borrow books from all over the United States which as a senior non-commissioned officer of the U.S. Army I was able to use all of the facilities of this wonderful library.

Thanks also, to Brother Keith Arrington, Assistant Librarian of the Iowa Masonic Library in Cedar Rapids, Iowa, operated by the Caucasian Grand Lodge A.F. & A.M. of Iowa. Mrs. Jean Hutson Blackwell, curator of the Schomburg Center for Research in Black Culture, New York Public Library, West 135th Street Branch which houses the Harry A. Williamson Prince Hall Masonic Collection. Also, John M. Sherman, Librarian, Caucasian Grand Lodge A.F. & A.M. of Massachusetts who assisted me, yet misjudged my intentions.

Special thanks also to Mrs. Virginia Ehlers of McLouth, Kansas for correcting the manuscript and above all, a special thank you to my wife Sandra, without whose support, this book could not have been completed.

A very special thanks to Brother L. Sherman Brooks of Jamestown, New York for designing the cover of this book and Mrs. Velma J. Best of Des Moines, Iowa who kindly corrected several pages. Above all else, a warm thank you to all Freemasons where-so-ever dispersed around the globe for taking the time to read my humble contribution to the literature of our profession.

JOSEPH A. WALKES, JR.

December, 1978

I

THE MASTER—PRINCE HALL

One cannot begin a serious work on Prince Hall Freemasonry without first presenting some facts concerning the man and the legend, responsible for the creation of the fraternity that bears his name. So much has been written about the Master, Prince Hall, one may wonder what purpose is served by rehashing the same story over and over, as it involves the early history of Masonry in America, which, in itself, is quite complex. As much as the writer would relish reviewing the early history of Masonry in Massachusetts, it is not within the present range of this work. In this chapter, the focus will be on Prince Hall himself.

In reviewing the early history of Freemasonry among Blacks, one must rely heavily on the numerous books that have been written on the subject. How much reliability the reader can place on these various works is questionable. The reader must rely on the writer's interpretation of events, and insofar as Prince Hall Masonry is concerned this reliance is quite risky.

Those who believe that "nothing establishes a fact until it has been verified," may very well wish to launch their own investigation. The field is far from being exhausted, and with continued research by those who seek to discover the full facts or merely to verify those that are now known, the material is available, and new discoveries are waiting to be unearthed.

The beginnings of Masonry among Blacks are surrounded by controversy, mystery, and passion, and, unfortunately, the record of its early events contains untruths. Harry E. Davis, the Prince Hall Masonic historian, wrote that "one of the saddest things about controversy is that it frequently obscures every other element concerning the topic except the point controverted. Colored Masonry has suffered much from the blight of controversy. In Masonic, as well as in political history, the Negro has been a vortex around which a veritable torrent of passion has whirled. In the midst of these tempests men do not take time to assemble and analyse simple facts, the scientific poise is lost, the historian is superseded by the advocate, and a wealth of information is neglected."(1)

In the preface to his book *The Beginning of Freemasonry in America* (1924), Melvin M. Johnson describes the care he took in collecting and checking all the information he used. Concerning some theories and unwarranted assertions that had been publicly made in the past and that had been copied and recopied by serious Masonic scholars, Brother Johnson declared that, "Nothing can justify the deliberate concealment of a reliable document or the publication of that which is manifestly fraudulent for the purpose of bolstering up an argument in support of some pet theory which the fraternity is asked to believe. Masonic students and historians, therefore, should be careful not to adopt without personal investigations, the conclusions arrived at by our best and most revered historians, except they are based upon a knowledge of the whole facts, including the recently discoverd evidence...Those who now or hereafter attempt to write Masonic history whether as to a single fact or a broad field, must be willing to subject themselves to the same tests applied to all other historians."(2)

As stated earlier, details of the early history of the beginning of Freemasonry among the Black man in the United States are easily attained, as hundreds of volumes, articles, pamphlets, letters, memorials, Grand Lodge proceedings, and documents have been printed. Unfortunately, most are incorrect; the works of the early historians are so thoroughly saturated with falsehoods as to render them almost valueless.

The dedicated Prince Hall Masonic historian, Harry A. Williamson, complied a bibliography giving about five hundred references to Prince Hall and Prince Hall Masonry, (3) however every item must be approached with caution.

Prince Hall Masonry began with a remarkable individual, Prince Hall, a man who was a credit to his race, his country, universal Freemasonry and himself. When one considers the era in which he lived the conditions of the time, and the numerous handicaps that he and his fraters faced, he must stand among the great men of American history.

There is little doubt that even well meaning Prince Hall historians, as well as Caucasian Masonic historians, have repeated obvious concocted stories of Prince Hall's life. And in reality, what concerns his personal life has little or no bearing on his Masonry, or the Lodge that he founded, or the introduction of Freemasonry to the Black man.

The usually accepted accounts of his life have it that Prince Hall was born in Bridgetown, Barbados, British West Indies, on the 12th of September, 1748, the son of Thomas Prince Hall, an English leather merchant, and his wife, a free Negro woman of "French descent." After supposedly serving his apprenticeship in the leather trade, Prince Hall went to Boston, arriving in 1765 and by hard work he became a freeholder and a voter. He was converted to Methodism and became an ordained minister (4). All of which is untrue! A number of writers, like John E. Bruce, believed that "he was employed as a steward on one of the many vessels plying between Boston and England; and that the African Lodge evolved from a little club in Boston."(5) William H. Upton in his Prince Hall Letter Book pointed out that the State of Ohio claimed Prince Hall as a native son.

The generally accepted, but completely false, date of Prince Hall's birth is September 12, 1748. However, the death notices which appeared in six Boston newspapers, published Monday, December 7, 1807, point to his birth being in 1735.

Extract from "Boston Gazette":

DEATHS. On Friday morning, Mr. Prince Hall, aged 72, Master of the African Lodge. Funeral this afternoon, at 3 o'clock from his late dwelling house in Lendell's lane; which his friends and relatives are requested to attend without a more formal invitation.

Extract from "Independent Chronicle":

DEATHS. Mr. Prince Hall, aged 72, Master of the African Lodge. Funeral this afternoon at 3 o'clock from his late dwelling house in Lendell's Lane; which his friends are requested to attend without a more formal invitation.

It must be noted that Jeremy Belknap, the historian, wrote in his letter to Judge Tucker in 1795, "I am inclined to think that slaves were numerous before 1763, than at that time, because, in the two preceeding (sic) wars, many of them enlisted either into the army or on board vessels of war, with a view to procure their freedom. One of my informants, Prince Hall, a very intelligent black man, aged fifty-seven years, thinks that slaves were most numerous about the year 1745." This would indicate that Hall was born in 1738.(6) Harry E. Davis in his *Freemasonry Among Negroes* states that Grimshaw, the historian, who assigns 1748 as the correct date, claims to have secured it from headstones and vital statistics at Bridgetown in 1869. (7) Prince Hall in a Deposition for John Vinall dated August 31, 1807, declared: "I, Prince Hall of Boston in the Country of Suffolk, Leather Dresser and Laborer, aged about seventy years..."(8) Which would have made Hall's birth around 1737.

Using the January 14, 1787, Petition of African Blacks to General Court for aid in establishing an African Colony, which Prince Hall signed, as their basis, there are those who believe that Hall's place of birth was Africa. But it must be remembered that during this period the term "Negro" was seldom used by Blacks; hence such terms as "The African Church," "The African School," or "African Lodge" were more in keeping with what the Blacks considered themselves.

The *Philalethes* magazine of June, 1962 and April, 1963 contained two very interesting articles by John M. Sherman which must be mentioned. In the April, 1963 issue Sherman published a facsimile of an old notorial record which reads:

> "This may certify it is my concern that Prince Hall has lived with us 21 years and served us well upon all occassions for which reasons we maturely give him his freedom and that he is no longer to be reckoned a slave, but has been always accounted as a freeman by us as he has served us faithfully upon that account we have given him his freedom as Witness our hands this Ninth day of April 1770."
>
> Witness

Susannah Hall	William Hall
[Elizabeth Hall's mark]	Margaret Hall
	Boston 12th April, 1770

(*Author's Note:* Harold A. Wilson, Grand Historian of the Prince Hall Grand Lodge of New York in a letter dated March 1, 1965 to Mr. George E. Richter, reviewing the two articles written by Sherman for the *Philalethes*, found the manumission certificate as belonging to the Masonic Prince Hall to be "incredible, absurd and ridiculous," noting that there were a number of Prince Halls residing in or around Boston in 1749. Wilson also noted that the manumission document was not an original document, but rather a copy or transcript for the diary purpose of Ezekiel Price for his own non-official personal records. Wilson's letter, which is in the possession of this writer, refutes all of the writings of John Sherman, and is of interest to all students who want to investigate this period.)

For those who accept this document, this would place Hall from 1749 to 1770 as a servant in the family of William Hall. Sherman writes that William Hall was a respected citizen and property owner of Boston and had for a long time been known for his civic and philanthropic acts. He was a leather-dresser by trade and owned real estate, ten yards in the vicinity of what is now Post Office Square. He had been active in the Charitable Irish Society of Boston since 1737 and was the first elected President of the Society. William Hall died August 16, 1771, aged 75 years, and in his will specified the distribution of his property between his wife and children. He did not mention Prince Hall in the will, but it seems probable, according to Sherman, that he generously did what he could to set Prince up in business as a leather-dresser and gave him what was needed before he died or when he set him free. Besides, as Sherman points out, there was a law in Massachusetts against the manumission of slaves unless their master gave bonds that their estates and heirs should maintain them, in case of sickness or decrepitude, so that they might not become a burden to the public.(9)

So, in 1749, Prince Hall became a servant of William Hall and would have been about fourteen years old. Seven years later, in 1756, Primus Hall, who later would claim he was the son of Prince Hall, was born. Of Primus Hall, more will be discussed in the next chapter.

In the August 31, 1807, deposition of Prince Hall concerning John Vinal, he wrote, "I was a member of his church (Andrew Croswell), being in full communion therewith, for a number of years, having been received into the same in the year of our Lord one thousand seven hundred and sixty two in Nov'r."(10)

On the second day of November, 1763, Prince Hall was married and recorded in the Book of Marriages as:

Prince, neg. svt. William Hall & Sarah, neg. svt. Francis Richie.(11)

Three years later, Prince Hall's wife died and the headstone was engraved:

"Here lies ye Body of Sarah Ritchery Wife of Prince Hall died Feb. the 26th 1769 aged 24 years."(12)

In 1770, as has been shown, William Hall set him free, and it would seem that after his manumission, Hall went to Gloucester, where he married a Flora Gibbs, as the register of Boston Marriages shows:

"Prince Hall of Boston and Flora (Gibbs) of Gloucester Married by Rev. Samuel Chandler, August 22, 1770"(13)

On December 12, 1771, Prince Hall and his wife, Flora, filed a writ for damages against one Francis Norwood, Tide-Waiter of Gloucester, with the Sheriff of Essex County, for ten pounds. In this document, Prince Hall described himself as "a free Negro of said Boston, Leather-dresser."

From 1771 to 1776 there is a blank, as no records or documents have been located to establish the whereabouts of Prince Hall.

January 13, 1777, Prince Hall was one of the signers to a petition addressed to the Massachusetts Legislature asking for the abolition of slavery. The petition was from "a great number of Negroes who are detained in a state of slavery."

On April 24, 1777, he presented his bill for   1.19.0 to Col. Craft's Regt. of Artillery for "5 drumheads delivered at sundrey times."

The Boston Assessor's "Talking Books" show that Prince Hall was assessed for poll taxes and real estate taxes in 1780, 1784, 1786, 1787 as "Negro Grand Master to the Lodge"; 1788 as "Free Mason"; 1789, 1790, 1791, 1798, 1800, 1801 and 1803 as "Worshipful Grand Master." The tax lists were also used as voting lists, and they show that Prince Hall was eligible to vote in Boston. His eligibility is also shown by the fact that the historian mentioned earlier, Jeremy Belknap, wrote to Ebenezar Hazard that "Prince Hall, Grand Master of the Black Lodge, constantly votes for Governor and Representatives; so do some others."(14)

On January 14, 1787, Prince Hall signed a Petition of African Blacks to General Court for aid in establishing an African Colony; another "Petition of a great number of Blacks" was signed by Prince Hall, February 27, 1788.

In the Diary of William Bentley, D.D., Pastor of the East Church in Salem, a Freemason, recorded this incident:

> "July 11, 1801. A Turtle Feast of the Marine Society at Osgood's in South Fields. The Turtle was given by a gentleman in Havana. The Clergy was invited. Our chief cook was Prince Hall, an African, & a person of great influence upon his Colour in Boston, being Master of the African Lodge, & a person to whom they refer with confidence their principal affairs. The Clergy was introduced to him, & the principal gentlemen took notice of him. Brother Freeman of Boston pronounced him a very useful man & that the Masonic Negroes are evidently many grades above the common blacks of Boston. Prince Hall assures that he has lately published another, which he is to send me. His first Charge tho'not correct, was useful."(15)

On June 28, 1804, Prince Hall married Zilpha (or Zilpoy) Johnson. After his death, her name is shown as Silva(16) and she was appointed adminstratrix of his estate, which the appraisers valued at $47.22 on August 8, 1808.

Again, in the Diary of William Bentley, under the date September 20, 1807, there appears, "Prince Hall, the leading African of Boston & author of several Masonic addresses, tells me that an African preacher was in Boston who had been ordained by Bishop White of Philadelphia in the English forms." (17)

On August 31, 1807, four months before he died, Prince Hall made the following sworn deposition for John Vinal, a member of the Church of the Rev. Andrew Croswell:

"I, Prince Hall of Boston in the County of Suffolk, Leather Dresser and Laborer, aged about seventy years, do testify and say that I was well acquainted with the Rev'd Andrew Croswell, a minister of the Gospel in Boston who preached in the brick meeting house in School Street in sd. Boston, now taken down. I was a member of his church, being in full communication therewith, for a number of years, having been received into the same in the year of our Lord one thousand seven hundred and sixty two in Nov'r. and I continued a *1762* member of the same church in full communion therewith & partaking the Sacrament there until the said Rev'd Andrew Croswell died. I also very well remember that John Vinall, Esq. of Boston aforesaid, was admitted a member of the same church, after being propounded—this was about a year after my admission into the Church; and that he continued to receive the Sacrament there, as a member of the same church until the small pox took place in Boston, when Mr. Croswell left the town on account of that disorder and his church members were scattered; many of them leaving the town and going into the Country, and among them was the s'd John Vinall. This was about the year Seventeen hundred and sixty-three or sixty four, after which I do not know that the s'd. Vinall pertook of the Sacrament at R'd. Croswell's Church. (signed) Prince Hall(18)

As mentioned earlier, Prince Hall died December 4, 1807, and the notice of his death and funeral was published in six Boston newspapers. They agree that his age was 72 years, that he was Master of African Lodge, and that a Masonic ceremony was held. Sherman and others make a point to add that the death notices do not tell where the remains were interred, nor can this be found in the official city records. The grave of a former wife, Sarah Ritchery, who died February 26, 1769, is located in the Copp's Hill burying ground, and on the back side of this stone, the following epitaph to Prince Hall was added, evidently many years after he died.

"Here lies ye body of
Prince Hall
First Grand Master of the
Colored Grand Lodge of
Masons in Mass.

Died Dec. 7, 1807'

The date of death is incorrect.

In 1903 was published a so-called *Official history of Freemasonry Among The Colored People in North America*. This book was written by William Henry Grimshaw, Past Grand Master of the District of Columbia. Grimshaw was born August 4, 1847 or 48. His father's name was Robert Tyler and his mother's name was Julia Grimshaw. No explanation has been found for the reason he took the name of his mother. He worked for a number of years in the Bureau of Equipment and Commandant's Office, in the Navy Yard, was a doorkeeper in the Gallery of the House of Representatives, and was Library Assistant and Doorkeeper in the main reading room of the Library of Congress. He was a member of Social Lodge No. 1 in Washington, D.C. serving as its Worshipful Master, 1874-75. Social Lodge No. 1 was chartered on June 6, 1825, by the M.W. African Grand Lodge of North America in Philadelphia, Pennsylvania as Social Lodge No. 7. It became No. 1 on the rolls of the Grand Lodge of D.C., March 7, 1848 when this Grand Lodge was formed. Grimshaw served this Prince Hall Jurisdiction as Grand Master in 1907.

Grimshaw was probably well-meaning in his attempt to enlarge beyond the bounds of truth regarding Prince Hall's life. The stories cooked-up by him are inexcusable and cannot be justified. Such falsehood as Prince Hall's "being born in Bridgetown, Barbados on the 12th of September 1748, the son of Thomas Prince Hall, an English leather merchant and his wife a free Negro woman of French descent. After supposedly serving his apprenticeship in the leather trade, Prince Hall went to Boston, arriving in 1765, and by hard work became a free holder and a voter. He converted to Methodism and became an ordained minister."

All were figments of Grimshaw's overly active imagination and cannot be overlooked as an innocent stretching of the truth. These tales were accepted by Freemasonry, Black as well as White the world over, copied and recopied not only by the Craft, but by historians of Black history with the result that many of the falsehoods are recorded in these books and taught in Black study courses across the country, even to the point that some of it has found its way into the higher degrees of Prince Hall Freemasonry. That prominent Masonic historians and scholars, friends and enemies of Prince Hall Masonry, alike, were led astray by the deliberate fabrications by one individual, brings forth the lesson that Masonic research must be verified beyond a question and that nothing should be accepted at face value. And those who are found to falsify deliberately Masonic documentations, regardless of their good intentions, should be ostracized by the entire fraternity. The following from the Proceedings of the Prince Hall Grand Lodge of Massachusetts for 1906, page 82, is of interest:

"Reference is made to the portrait of Prince Hall. This is not known to be authentic, and the sketch of his life has little in the way of authenticity to commend it. In 1795 Prince Hall told the Rev. Dr. Belknap he was fifty-seven years of age, which would make the year of his birth 1738; Brother John D. Caldwell appears to quote Bro. William S. Gardner as saying that when initiated, March 8 (sic), 1775, Prince Hall was 32 years, 3 months and 28 days old, which would make the date of birth, Nov. 9, 1742; and Bro. Bruce (John Edward "Bruce Grit: Bruce") quotes Bro. Grimshaw—who really did not know anything about it—as saying, Sept. 12, 1748. Our preference is for the year 1738, being based upon Hall's statement to Belknap. ...How a supposedly intelligent man can write such nonsense, and other supposedly intelligent men seriously quote it, passes all comprehension."

During the Revolutionary War it is claimed that Prince Hall headed a committee of freemen to General Washington's headquarters seeking to join the Army;(19) and that Prince Hall served in the Continental Army. There are three records of soldiers bearing the name:

Prince Hall, Dartmouth. List of men who marched from Dartmouth camp under command of Capt. Benjamin Dillingham and arrived there Feb. 15, 1776; also, Private, Capt. Joshua Wilbore's Co., Col. Ebenzor Francis's regt; pay abstract for travel allowance from camp home, etc; said Hall credited with allowance for 3 days (65 miles); company drafted from Taunton, Raynham, Easton, Dartmouth, Freetown, Berkley, and Dighton; warrant allowed in Council Nov. 29, 1776.

Prince Hall, Medford, Receipt dated Medford, May 25, 1778, for bounty paid said Hall by Richard Hall, in behalf of the town of Medford, to serve in the Continental Army; also, descriptive list of men raised in Middlesex Co. for the term of 9 months from the time of their arrival at Fishkill, agreeable to resolve of April 20, 1778; Capt. Brook's Co., Col. Thatcher's regt., age, 30 yrs.; stature, 5 ft. 3 in.; residence, Medford; engaged for town of Medford; arrived at Fishkill June 21, 1778; also, list of men returned as received of Jonathan Warner, Commissioner, by Col. R. Putname, July 20, 1778.

Prince Hall, Medford (also Medfiled). List of men raised to serve in the Continential Army from 1st Middlesex Co., regt., as returned by Lieut. Stephen Hall, dated Medford, Feb. 19, 1778, residence, Medford; engaged for town of Medford; joined Capt. Allen's Co., Col. Bailey's regt., term, during war; also, list of men mustered by Nat. Barbar, Muster Master for Suffolk Co., dated Boston, April 13, 1777; also, Private 3d co., Col. John Bailey's regt.; Continental Army pay accounts for service from April 7, 1777, to Dec. 18, 1777;

residence, Medfield; reported died Dec. 18, 1778; also, (late) Capt. Jacob Allen's (3d) Co., Col. Bailey's regt.; return of men in service before Aug. 15, 1777; also, same Co., and regt., company return dated Camp at Valley Forge, Jan. 24, 1778; also, Capt. Adams Bailey's (late Capt. Jacob Allen's) co., Col. Bailey's (2d); muster roll made up from Jan. 1, 1777, to Jan. 1, 1780; enlisted April 7, 1777. (20)

It is this writer's contention that Grimshaw was inspired not only by the above records, but also the records of Primus Hall, a Revolutionary War hero, who claimed to be the son of Prince Hall. We shall meet Primus Hall in the next chapter.

But Masonically, it is immaterial whether or not Prince Hall served in the Army. Of the three Prince Halls mentioned the problem becomes one of identification. One of the Halls is listed as having died in service. Of the remaining two, not much is really known of the Prince Hall from Dartmouth.

In Charles Brooks' *History of the Town of Medford, Middlesex County, Massachusetts*, etc. (p. 438) he writes:

"In 1754, there were in Medford twenty-seven male and seven female slaves, and fifteen free blacks; total, forty-nine. In 1764, there were forty-nine free blacks. When the law freed all the slaves, many in Medford chose to remain with their masters, and they were faithful unto death."

In 1754, there were four slaves belonging to the Hall families. Benjamin Hall had a slave named Prince who died in 1766. In 1772, Stephen Hall had a servant named Prince who married Chloe, a Negro servant of Richard Hall (Medford Vital Records).

In Helen Tilden Wild's book *Medford in the Revolution*, she describes the role of the people of Medford during the war. Of the second Prince Hall, Miss Wild writes:

"Hall, Prince, Enlisted for 3 yrs., April 7, 1777; died Dec. 18, 1778: vol. 7, p. 105. Rev. Osgood records in his diary, April 1, 1777, "Prince ran away last night." Mr. Osgood at that time boarded with Mr. Richard Hall, whose negro servant, Chloe, married Prince, a negro servant of Stephen Hall, Eeq., Sept. 15, 1772."

Of the first Prince Hall, Miss Wild writes:

"Hall, Prince. Enlisted for 9 mos., 1778, age 30; vol. 7, p. 105. Receipt signed by himself for bounty received on enlistment can be seen at state archives. Free negro; taxed in Medford, 1778 and 1779; he was the author of a petition to the House of Representatives urging the abolition of slavery in Massachusetts. He

was the founder of Free Masonry among Negroes, receiving his degrees from a
military lodge, consisting of British soldiers in Boston, March 6, 1775. Married
Phebe, a slave of Mrs. Lydie Bowman Baker, of Boston, who set her free. Their
home was on Phillips Street, Boston, where he died Dec. 7, 1807. See archives of
Prince Hall Grand Lodge F. & A.M.

The problem remains as stated before, one of identification.
Benjamin Quarles makes a good point when he wrote that, "A final
problem has been the determination of Negro identity. Since most of
the participants in the Revolutionary War were racially anonymous,
on what basis may a person be identified as a Negro? In this work I
have designated an individual as a Negro only when the source
specifically states it or where the source is referring only to Negroes. I
make only one assumption: if the first or last name of a person was
Negro, he was not likely to be white. Although there are certain
names largely confined to Negroes, I have not assumed that persons
with such names were colored. Thus, although three of the Americans
on the sloop *Charming Polly*, captured by the British on May 16,
1777, bore the typically Negro names of William Cuff, Prince Hall
and Cuff Scott (and all came from Massachusetts coastal towns,
where Negro seamen were common), I have not assumed that they
were Negroes." (21) This rationale can also be used with identifying a
Prince Hall, as being the Masonic Prince Hall. So in a manner of
speaking there is no proof at this writing that the Masonic Prince Hall
served in the Revolutionary War, nor is there any proof that he did
not.

It is generally accepted that Freemasonry among Blacks in the
United States began with the initiation of Prince Hall and fourteen
other "free" Blacks in Lodge No. 441, Irish Constitution, attached to
the 38th Regiment of Foot, British Army garrisoned at Castle
Williams (now Fort Independence), Boston Harbor on 6 March 1775,
the Master of the Lodge being one Sergeant J. Batt (or J.T. Batt or
John Batt.)

There are documents showing that a John Batt was discharged from
the 38th Regiment of Foot at Staten Island, New York, on the third of
February 1777, and that he was later enlisted in the Continental Army, Col. David Henly's Regiment on February 20, 1778, and deserted
June 10, 1778.

It is claimed that when the British Army left Boston, that Hall was
left a "permit" to meet as a Lodge, but apparently not to confer
degrees. Masonic authorities agree that this was how Africian Lodge

No. 1 was organized, and that Prince Hall later petitioned the Mother Grand Lodge of the world, England, for a warrant that was issued on September 29, 1784, for African Lodge 459.

In order to measure the greatness of Prince Hall, one must review the written documents left by him, his petitions to the Senate and House of Representatives of Massachusetts, his Letter Book and his Charges to African Lodge. There has not been on the American Masonic scene, or in the pages of its history, so unique a Black Freemason as Prince Hall. His lack of a formal education, his bondage, and the racial conditions of the time merely enhance the character of this outstanding individual. His many accomplishments must be viewed in this light and his achievements in overcoming all of these handicaps, and the abuses, mistreatment and often viciousness that was heaped on him, his Lodge, and later the fraternity he founded, is more than proof that Prince Hall was indeed "The Master."

This brief summary will lead us into the next chapter which deals with Primus Hall, who was not a Freemason, yet whose name invariably appears in the Grimshaw tales of Prince Hall.

REFERENCES FOR PART I

1. Harry E. Davis, *A History of Freemasonry Among Negroes in America* (United Supreme Council, A.A.S.R. Northern Jurisdiction, U.S.A., Inc.—Prince Hall Affiliation-1946), p.5. Davis, himself a Prince Hall Masonic scholar without equal, did not stick to his own commandment as a number of avoidable errors appear in this otherwise brilliant book.

2. Melvin M. Johnson, *The Beginnings of Freemasonry in America* (The Masonic Service Association of the United States, 1924), p. viii.

3. Harry A. Williamson, *The Negro Mason in Literature* (author's collection, microfilm, 1929).

4. William H. Grimshaw, *Official History of Freemasonry Among the Colored People in North America* (New York, Macoy Publishing and Masonic Supply Co., 1903), p. 69. Though this work contains many fabrications concerning the life and times of Prince Hall, there remains a wealth of material concerning the later establishment of individual Prince Hall Grand Lodges, though it is best to verify all facts presented by Grimshaw.

5. John Edward (Bruce Grit) Bruce, *Prince Hall the Pioneer of Negro Masonry—Proofs of the Legitimacy of Prince Hall Masonry* (author's collection, 1921), p. 4. This is an interesting pamphlet, but for the most part follows the Grimshaw fabrications. Yet he emphasizes "the great importance and need of keeping historical records and correct biographical sketches of the important men in the order, the dates of their birth and death, and wherever possible, their photographs, so that in the coming years the boys of today, who will be the Master Masons of tomorrow, will have the data at hand from which to write the history of Negro Masonry in the Centuries to come."

6. Jeremy Belknap, *Queries respecting the Slavery and Emancipation of Negroes in Massachusetts, proposed by the Hon. Judge Tucker of Virginia, and answered by the Rev. Dr. Belknap* (author's collection, 1795), p. 199.

7. Davis, *op. cit.*, p. 266. I am not sure where Davis got his information.

8. Suffolk Country Registry of Deeds-1807, August 31, Prince Hall, Grantor—Deposition of Prince Hall Concerning John Vinall, member of Church of the Rev. Andrew Croswell on School Street. Vol. 221, p. 10.

9. John M. Sherman, unpublished manuscript (author's collection, 1967).

10. Suffolk Country Registry of Deeds, *op. cit.*

11. Boston Marriages, 1752-1809 (Boston Record Commissioners), p. 422.

12. Davis, *op. cit.*, p. 16.

13. Boston Marriages, *op. cit.*, p. 299 (Gloucester).

14. Davis, *op. cit*, p. 16, Belknap Papers (1788), p. 12. Collections Mass. Hist. Soc. Vol. IV (author's collection).

15. The Diary of William Bentley, D.D., Vol. 2, p. 279 (author's collection).

16. Suffolk Registry of Probate, v. 106, p. 394 (author's collection).

17. Bentley, *op. cit.*

18. Suffolk County Registry of Deeds, *op. cit.*

19. Grimshaw, *op. cit*, p. 74.

20. *Massachusetts Soldiers and Sailors in the War of the Revolution,* Vol. VII, 1891, p. 105.

21. Benjamin Quarles, *The Negro in the American Revolution* (Durham, N.C., University of North Carolina Press, 1961), p. xi.

22. Davis, *op. cit.*, p. 21.

II

THE STORY OF A WATCH CHAIN

It is sad, indeed, to see how Prince Hall Masonic history is often intentionally twisted and distorted; and even childhood recollections or hearsay are accepted as fact without anyone carefully verifying the information by comparing it with known facts, official records and documents. As brought out in the last chapter in the case of Helen Tilden Wild's book, *Medford in the Revolution,* concerning the identification of one of the Prince Halls, the data were supplied to her from a source that should have been reliable, the Prince Hall Grand Lodge of Massachusetts. Throughout Prince Hall Masonry, even before the Grimshaw fabrications and inventions, the fraternity has been plagued with half-truths, legends, and myths, often by well-meaning individuals, who frequently created more yarns. The mere fact that the Grimshaw manufactured untruths have found their way into the higher degrees is an example. The fact that fables such as the one recorded below was produced in the proceedings of a Grand Lodge that was issued to mark an historic occasion shows the abuse of distortions.

Daniel Thomas Vose Huntoon, a Caucasian Freemason from the Caucasian Grand Lodge of Massachusetts, wrote a letter to Past Grand Master Lewis Hayden of The Prince Hall Grand Lodge of Massachusetts in 1883. The letter concerned the story of a gift of a gold chain, which he claimed belonged to Phoebe, "the wife of Prince Hall."

P.G.M. Hayden accepted the story. He was so impressed with it that the letter was reproduced in the proceedings of the Grand Lodge commemorating the One Hundreth Anniversary of the granting of Warrant 459 to African Lodge, which was held in Boston, September 29th, 1884. It has always been this writer's contention that the history of Prince Hall Masonry should be researched and written by the

Prince Hall Mason himself, who, having knowledge of Black history, could produce verified accounts of Black Masonic history. The two are not separate or apart, but a unit of the same. The history of Prince Hall Freemasonry is the history of the Black man in America, and most of the events recorded in Black America are found in the proceedings of the individual Grand Lodges. As a rule, Prince Hall Freemasons played some role. Statements of facts from those outside of, as well as those within, Prince Hall Freemasonry should be taken with a grain of salt. Above all, Prince Hall Freemasonry should beware of those bearing gifts. The letter as printed in the proceedings reads:

STORY OF A WATCH CHAIN

Mr. Lewis Hayden, Past Grand Master of the Prince Hall Grand Lodge of Free and Accepted Masons.

My Dear Sir, You asked me to put into permanent shape the story I told you of the chain which I wore on the day I informed you of its history. I will do so, that it may be preserved in the archives of Prince Hall Grand Lodge of Masons.

In the year 1729, the Rev. Jonathan Bowman, son of Capt. Joseph Bowman of Lexington, who had five years before graduated with distinction from Harvard College, was called by the ancient church in Dorchester as colleague to the Rev. John Danforth. He was duly ordained in November of the year above mentioned; and shortly after married Elizabeth Hancock, daughter of Rev. John Hancock, commonly styled "Bishop" on account of his ecclesiastical prominence. Her mother was the daughter of the Rev. Thomas Clark; she was the sister of Thomas Hancock, who built the famous house which stood on Beacon Street, subsequently the Governor's residence.

Soon after his marriage, Jonathan Bowman purchased, in 1730, land that had formerly been a portion of the Gov. Stoughton homestead, and upon it erected a house, which still stands upon Savinhill Avenue in Dorchester. Here were born to the young clergyman and his wife five children; and when on the 16th of December, 1741, the sixth claimed a family conference as to what name it should bear, it was decided that the new-comer should be called Lydia, in honor of Lydia Henchman, who had married Thomas Hancock.

The following interesting episode of her early life is taken from an article in the Boston "Transcript," May 21, 1883. "She belonged to a highly respectable family, and had many personal attractions, consequently many suitors. Among them was John Wiswell, a young man of about her age, belonging to a very respectable family in the same neighborhood, who aspired to some consideration in her list of lovers, and published his claim by perpetuating their names on stone. This stone as I recollect it (and I have examined many times, and pointed it out to my children as a reminiscence of their great-grand-mother) was about four feet long, and very irregular in shape, except on one side which was very smooth and flat; its thickness was about fourteen inches, it stood on Old Hill, now Savin Hill, which in old times was a favorite stroll for young people on moonlight nights. The inscription was simply, "Lydia Bowman, John Wiswell."

But Lydia was better pleased with a young gentleman who, graduating from Harvard College in 1760, determined to enter the ministry, and sought from her father the instruction necessary for such a life. From a daily visitation their acquaintance soon ripened into friendship, then into love; and in 1769 she was married to James Baker. On her wedding day she was presented by her parents, as a portion of her marriage dowry, with a female slave; a bright honest and intelligent girl.

Slavery was an existing institution in Massachusetts, at this period and Phoebe, for that was the colored girl's name, had been born and brought up in the family of her young mistress, and was the most valuable gift the worthy clergyman could have given his daughter as a wedding present. Mr. James Baker, my great-grandfather, the bridegroom, lived in a house still standing at the corner of Washington and Centree Street, opposite the Town Hall, in Dorchester. In my boyhood days, the daughter, Miss Lydia Baker, occupied this homestead; she was, when a child, as fondly loved and cared for by Phoebe as her brother Edmund. Mr. James Baker was a gentlemen of the old school, who was in the habit of giving dinner-parties to his friends. Deeming his staff of servants inadequate, he, on one grand occasion, sent to Boston for Prince Hall, who, though a man of wealth "sufficient," as Baker says, "to vote in town-meetings," was not above going out to wait upon the table and assist at gentlemens' dinner parties. In this respect he resembled, as he did in character and standing, the late celebrated colored caterer of modern times, Mr. Joshua B. Smith, the friend of Sumner. Mr. Hall was fond of the conversation of refined and cultivated gentlemen; and it was a pleasure to him to stand behind the host during the repaste, and listen to the wit and wisdom that fell from the lips of guests.

He was a respectable, honest, and industrious man, and was the most prominent colored man of his day; subsequently Master of the African Lodge, which now bears his name; and active, in 1771, in petitioning the General Court to abolish slavery in this State; and ask for the passage of an act whereby his people "may be restored to the enjoyment of that freedom which is the natural love of all men, and their children who were born in this land of liberty may not be held as slaves after they arrive at the age of twenty-one years."

On the occasion of the dinner which he was to superintend, Phoebe, the young colored girl, was enlisted in his service; and Hall was so much pleased with her ability and winning manners that he asked permission to call on her, the result of which was that he made her a proposal of marriage, which Phoebe accepted. Her master gave his consent, and gave freedom to her; and she became the wife of Prince Hall.

But when the time came for her to leave the old house, where she had been so well treated, for slavery in Massachusetts was a totally different aspect from Southern slavery, Phoebe's heart was very sad. The little money that she had saved from time to time, she had invested, as was the custom before the days of savings banks, in a gold bead. One by one the number increased, until a complete circle of shining spheres, each the size of a large pearl, encircled her dusky throat. It was all the property she had in the world. So she was married from the old homestead, like one of the family, and went to the house of her husband on what is now Phillips Street, Boston. Phoebe knew how to make it comfortable, how to make her husband happy, and how to advance his position in society; and whenever her old mistress drove to see her, she was warmly welcomed by the former slave, and treated with great respect and propriety by Mr. Hall.

During the time she had lived in the family, two children had been born to James Baker; a son named Edmund, and a daughter Lydia. They were tenderly cared for by Phoebe during the period of their infancy and childhood. The attachment was mutual. It was while in charge of these children that an anecdote is related of Phoebe that shows there was a bit of the love of fun in her make-up. Mr. Edmund J. Baker, now living in Dorchester, to whom I am indebted for the facts in this story, thus tells it:

"Mr. John Jones, a wealthy Boston merchant, died Sept. 10, 1772, and left his widow in affluence, occupying the place subsequently lived in for several years by Daniel Webster, now known as the Webster Gardens, in Dorchester. When Phoebe's work was done, she used to get permission to take one of her children over to Madam Jones to spend the evening; and I have heard my father tell how the servants of Madam Jones would get King the coachman to take a party of them in the booby-hut for a sleigh-ride, unbeknown to the old lady."

King was a very pious Royalist, and never forgot in his prayers King George and all the royal family, and would add to the force of his prayer by beseeching God "to damn George Washington and the Continential Congress."

Years rolled away, and Phoebe was in the habit of making visits to the children and grandchildren of her old friends. About seventy years ago Phoebe spent several days at the house of Mr. Edmund Baker, who was born April 20, 1770, and died Oct. 11, 1846, whom she had nursed in childhood, where were two children bearing the names so dear to her in earlier years, Edmund James, born Nov. 15, 1804, and still living, and Lydia Bowman Baker. So strong was her interest, that to the latter she gave as a souvenir of past memories the string of gold beads that she wore on her wedding day. In the change of fashions, beads were no longer worn. Lydia had them made into a gold chain, which she attached to her watch, and wore it around her neck as long as she lived, in remembrance of Phoebe the slave and the friend. On July 7, 1841, Lydia was married to the Rev. Benjamin Huntoon; and when she died Oct. 2, 1884, the chain was considered as too fragile for a man; and I therefore took the larger part, in 1869, to a Jeweler on Washington Street, in Boston, in whom I had every confidence. I told him the story of the gold in the chain, that it was a precious heirloom, that I wanted it melted in a separate crucible, and gave him a design for a strong chain. I saw it several times during the time it was being manufactured, and know that the jeweler did not deceive me.

I told you that money could not buy the chain, but as you desired to have in the archives of your lodge a piece of gold that was once owned by the wife of Prince Hall, I have cut from the chain which my mother had made, a link, which you will find accompanying this letter. I have now fullfilled the promise I made you, and given you the history of my watchchain.

There is no man in this country whose memory is held in greater respect by the colored people for his labors of philanthropy and patriotism than Prince Hall. If this souvenir of his wife, with its strange history, shall add any thing to the interest of bygone days, you are cordially welcome to it. Yours very truly;

D.T.V. HUNTOON

Canton, April 20, 1883

A touching narration, but the evidence is clear that Grand Master Hayden was deceived. Grimshaw also wrote that "Prince Hall married after the war Miss Phoebe Baker, a bright and intelligent girl."

The truth of the matter was that *Phoebe was never the wife of Prince Hall*, the founder of Prince Hall Masonry, but the wife of another man, *Primus Hall*, a Revolutionary War hero, born February 29, 1756 and who died March 22, 1842.

The public records of the Boston Marriages from 1752 to 1809 list under the year 1784 the following:

> Primus Trash Watt & Phoebe (sic) Robson (free negros)
> int. reads (Primus Trusk Hall) (Phoebe).(4)

The date of this marriage was May 2, 1784. At this date Primus would have been 28 years old, and Phoebe 23. Prince Hall would have been 49. (5) Verification of Phoebe's age appeared in her obituary printed in the *Columbian Centinel*, Wednesday, December 21, 1808, page 3, which reads as follows:

> On Sunday, Mrs. Phoebe, Wife of Mr. Primus Hall, AET 47: Funeral tomorrow afternoon, at 3 o'clock from his house in Southack-Street.

There is also a public record of the inventory of the Estate of Prince Hall to the Suffolk Country Probate Court. Sylvia Hall, the widow and adminstrator of the estate presented this inventory which the appraiser valued at $47.22 on August 15th, 1808, four months after Phoebe's death.

It is quite obvious that there is some confusion over Prince Hall, the Freemason, and Primus Hall, as can be seen by the following *incorrect* statement which appeared in Grimshaw's *Official History*.

> As to Primus Hall being the son of Prince Hall, this is not true, because he was as old as Prince Hall. When he signed the petition Feb. 27, 1799, he was then fifty-nine years old and as further proof, Prince Hall was not married until 1784. (6)

The petition that Grimshaw refers to was submitted to the House and Senate of Massachusetts by Prince Hall when a number of African Lodge members and other freemen of New England were carried off on a ship to be sold into slavery.

In order to untangle some of the confusion between the two men, one merely needs to go to the public records and, in so doing, learn of the life of a most interesting non-Masonic Black Revolutionary War hero. Primus Hall was an obvious acquaintance of Prince Hall and also *a son by some one who bore the same name.* The following is taken from the public records of the Veterans Administration:

PRIMUS HALL (7)

You are advised that it appears from the papers in the Revolutionary War pension claim, W 751, that Primus Hall (the name appears as Primus Trask) the son of Prince, a freeman of color and Delia, who was a servant in the family of a Mr. Walker, was born February 29, 1756, at the home of said Walker, on Beacon Steet, Boston, Massachusetts. When he was one month old, he was given to Ezra Trask, then a resident of Beverly, Essex County, Massachusetts, and later of Danvers, Massachusetts, and was brought up by him but never considered by him as a slave, and when fifteen years of age, Mr. Trask gave him his freedom from his apprenticeship as a shoemaker.

While residing in Danvers, Massachusetts, he enlisted early in January, 1776, served as a private in Captain Joseph Butler's Company, Colonel John and Thomas Nixon's Massachusetts Regiment, was in the retreat from Govenor's Island, in skirmishes at Rattlesnake Hill, Harlem Heights, Mile Square and in the battles of White Plains, Trenton and Princeton, in which last named engagement he captured two British soldiers, single handed, chasing them over a half mile, and was discharged after a service of one year and six weeks.

He enlisted in 1777, exact date not given, served in Captain Samuel Flint's Company, Colonel Johnson's Massachusetts Regiment, was at the second battle of Stillwater, was at his captain's side and caught him when he fell mortally wounded at that engagement, and at the capture of Burgoyne, length of service three months. It was stated that he acted as waiter to Captain Flint.

He enlisted in 1778, served as a private in Captain Woodbury's Company of Massachusetts Troops, marched to Rhode Island, where he assisted in building a fort, was detached and served with the French sappers and miners, entire length of this service three months.

In the years 1781 and 1782, he served twenty-two months as steward to Colonel Timothy Pickering, Commissary General of the Army, and was with him at the siege of Yorktown.

He was allowed pension by special act of Congress, approved June 28, 1838. He was at that time a resident of Boston, Massachusetts. He died March 22, 1842, in Boston, Massachusetts.

He was a soapboiler and accumulated real and personal property worth over $6,000. Silas Trask, who had reared him, became in his old age infirm and poor, and Primus very generously contributed to his support.

The soldier married October 29, 1817, Anna or Ann Clark. Their marriage was recorded in the town records of Boston, Massachusetts [nine years after the death of Phoebe].

Soldier's widow, Ann, was allowed pension on her application executed June 21, 1853, at which time she was aged sixty-two years and resided in Boston, Massachusetts. A little later in the same year she was residing in Somerville, Middlesex County, Massachusetts, and in 1855, was still residing at the last named place.

There is no reference to children.
This history to be
furnished if ever
called for.
It was written just
to have a record of
negroes.

Primus Hall died on March 22, 1842, and the following obituary appeared in the March 25 issue of *The Daily Atlas of Boston* page 2, column 7:

In this city, 22d inst. Primus Hall, a respectable colored citizen, and a Revolutionary pensioner of the U.S., aged 84. Mr. Hall was well known, particularly the younger portion of our citizens, to whom he was in the habit of recounting scenes of the Revolutionary War, especially the capture of Gen. Burgoyne and the surrender of Lord Cornwallis, at both of which he was present. He was attached to the Quartermaster General Department, and for about 2 years was in the military family of Genl. Washington, of whom he spoke with that fervor of attachment which was common to all who were personally acquainted with that great man. He has departed full of years to meet, we trust, the reward of a good and faithful servant.

As can be seen by the official records herein presented, Primus Hall was an outstanding Black man. That he knew the *Masonic* Prince Hall can be seen by his signature appearing with Prince Hall on the petition to the House and Senate of Massachusetts, dated February 27, 1788. That he was the son of the *Masonic* Prince Hall is *doubtful*, and his only connection with Prince Hall Freemasonry was in the imagination of Daniel Thomas Vose Huntoon.

This chapter strays from the general nature of this work, but only for the purpose of showing how readily untruths are often accepted; and yet, how simple it is to take the time to research and verify certain allegations. How Lewis Hayden, himself, a Masonic scholar and historian could have accepted Huntoon's story cannot be explained, other than by the fact that he wanted to believe it. He wanted something of value, something of Prince Hall, a "discovery" of something new that was a link to the past. The same can be said of Grimshaw, The Prince Hall Grand Lodge of Massachusetts, and others who wanted an association with the past. Freemasonry supplied the Black man with a history that was radically different from the traditional one that he had been taught to accept. The importance of such an historical linkage to "free" men of colour, to the American

Revolutionary War, to a Charter from the Mother Grand Lodge of England, the alleged parentage of Prince Hall being an Englishman and a free Negro woman of French descent was an escape from the whole history of Negro servitude in America.

Prince Hall Masonry had a distinct, bold and glorious history of its own which was a psychological uplift to the Black man. But the sad part of it all is that so much attention has been given to the Grimshaw tales, when in fact Prince Hall Masonic history can stand on its own, without any exaggerations attached to it.

REFERENCES FOR PART II

1. Proceedings of the One Hundreth Anniversary of the Granting of Warrant 459 to African Lodge at Boston, Mass., Monday, Sept. 29, 1884 under the Auspices of the M.W. Prince Hall Grand Lodge F. & A.M. Mass., Thomas Thomas, Grand Master (Boston: Franklin Press, Rand, Avery and Company, 1885), p. 34.

2. William H. Grimshaw, *Official History of Freemasonry Among the Colored People in North America* (New York: Macoy Publishing & Masonic Supply Co., 1903), p. 83.

3. RG-15 Records of the Veterans Administration, Revolutionary War Pension Application File, W751, of Primus Hall (name also appears as Primus Trask), The National Archives and Records Service, General Service Administration, Washington, D.C. 20408.

4. A Volume of Records Relating to the Early History of Boston, containing Boston Marriages from 1752 to 1809, City Document No. 101, page 342, Year 1784.

5. Extracts from the *Boston Gazette* and extract from the *Independent Chronicle Death Notices, Monday, December 7th, 1807 cited in Chapter I*. Both cite Prince Hall's birth in 1735 and his death the 4th of December 1807.

6. Grimshaw, *op. cit.*, p. 83.

7. RG-15, Records of the Veteran's Administration, *op. cit.*

8. Primus Hall's estate was probated and valued at $9,708.06.

9. D.T.V. Huntoon was a son (one of 9 children) of Rev. Benjamin Huntoon, who was Grand Chaplain of the Grand Lodge of Massachusetts for five years beginning in 1827 and later served in several other Grand Lodge offices. D.T.V. Huntoon was at one time Master of a Lodge in Norfolk County.

III

JOHN MARRANT—BROTHER CHAPLAIN

In the early days of Prince Hall Masonry, there was a wayfaring Black Missionary who is recorded briefly in Black Masonic history as bringing a spiritual influence to the North American Indian and Prince Hall's African Lodge as well. Prince Hall Masonry is indebted to the research efforts of William H. Upton, P.G.M., of the Caucasian Grand Lodge of Washington, author of *Negro Masonry, Being a Critical Examination Among The Negroes of America* (1902), for a brief glimpse of the Masonic life of John Marrant, Brother Chaplain.

In the printed *Transactions* of the Quatuor Coronati Lodge Number 2076, Volume XIII of January, 1900, under the title of *The Prince Hall Letter Book* and listed as entry number 21, is a copy of a letter from Prince Hall to R. Holt, Deputy Grand Master of the Grand Lodge of England, dated June 4, 1789.

> "Received into the Lodge since August, two members, namely John Bean and John Marrant, a Black Minister from home, but last from Branchtown, Nova Scotia." (1)

There is also under entry number 27, Prince Hall's Letter to Lady Huntington (2) to "convey his humble thanks for the labors of John Marrant," and, "We, the members of African Lodge, have made him a member of that honorable society, and Chaplain of the same, which will be a great help to him in his travels, and may do a great deal of good to society." (3)

It is known that Brother Marrant preached a sermon before African Lodge 459 on June 24, 1789, and it may very well have been the first published speech by a Black American. Marrant's *Journal* privately printed in London by J. Taylor and Company at the Royal Exchange, circa 1788, is a chronicle of his selfless toil and endless journeyings to remote places, of passionate sermons to gatherings of black, white and red. Marrant had been helped by "Mr. Prince Hall, at whose house I lodged, one of the most respected characters in Bostontown."

While in London, he told the story of his life to the Reverend William Aldridge, who "arranged, corrected, and published" it. "John's narrative," commented *The Monthly Review* of London, "is embellished with a good deal of *adventure*, enlivened by the *marvelous*, and a little touch of the *miraculous...*" *The Narrative of the Life of John Marrant* was reprinted nineteen times during the next forty years (4) and placed Brother Marrant's name "high in the annals of service like the Jesuits of old, who spread the seed of Christianity among the American Indians before the birth of the American Republic, right on the soil where they had been born and reared in plain view of the cruelties and sufferings meted out to their African forbears (sic)." (5)

John Marrant was born in New York City on June 15, 1765. The biographer of Marrant, The Reverend Mr. Aldridge (6), states that he was taken by his mother when five years old to Saint Augustine where he was sent to school, "and taught to read and spell." From listening to sermons preached by Missionaries, Marrant received inspiration and devoted his life to Christianity. By constant and patient study, he became an itinerant preacher among his fellow Blacks. His biographer records that an Indian hunter befriended him and taught him to speak his Indian language. With this, he became welcome among the Indian tribes in and around the state of New York where he converted to Christianity the "King" of the Cherokee Nation and his daughter. When the American Revolution came, Brother Marrant had carried the Gospel into the ranks of the Cherokee, Creek, Catawar and Housaw Indians. (7)

He fought against the Colonists by joining the English as a sailor on board the *"Princess Amelia"* and participated in an engagement of Dogger Bank on the fifth of August, 1781. He served six years and eleven months with the British Navy.

He was ordained on May 15, 1785, in London, England six months before the Reverend Lemuel Haynes, who many believed to be the first ordained Black of North America. Haynes was a Revolutionary War Minuteman who became a pastor of a Caucasian Congregation in Torrington, Connecticut later in 1785. (8)

Marrant's sermon preached to the African Lodge when he was thirty-four years old may be the high point of his checkered career.

He had not much longer to live, missed his English friends, and yearned to return to London. For the next six months he prayed and exhorted in Massachusetts. On February 5, 1790, a company of Black Bostonians, headed by Prince Hall, walked with him "down to the ship, with heavy hearts." A year later his coffin was lowered into a grave of the Burial Grounds on Church Street in Islington, a borough of London. (9) He is listed on the Roster of African Lodge No. 459, 1775-1809 (compiled from the old Ledger of African Lodge 459) and his name appears in the Proceedings of the Prince Hall Grand Lodge of Massachusetts, 1901, as "Rev'd John Morant (sic)." (10) The Tax List (Names of the Inhabitants of the Town of Boston, 1790, Census) Reprinted in Boston Record Commissioners Report, Vol. 22, page 507 for August 20th, shows the name "Prince Hall" following the name "Marant."

Like Marrant, there were others who came under the influence of Prince Hall and became well known Prince Hall Freemasons. Prince Saunders, Richard Allen, Absalom Jones, and James Forten, to name but a few, are briefly presented herein to point out the often forgotten historical fact that Prince Hall Masons played a major role in the building of Black America.

Prince Saunders, a member of Prince Hall's African Lodge, appears in the autobiography of William Bentley Fowle:

> "But to return to Saunders. He became engaged to a daughter of Paul Cuffee, a colored sea captain of New Bedford who owned several vessels, and S. would probably have married her, had he not been taken sick. He was tired of teaching, and wished to see England, and being ill, though not so ill as he pretended, he persuaded his friends to subscribe enough to enable him to go to London. Previously to going, he released Miss Cuffee from her engagement, and procured a white teacher for the school. *He carried good letters to England, and going as a delegate of the Masonic Lodge of Africans, who held their charter from England, he became acquainted with the Royal Duke who was at the head of the craft* there, and immediately was introduced to the highest circles. The nobility walked arm in arm with him in the streets of London." (11)

Saunders, who had studied at Dartmouth, became a teacher in the African School in Boston and was initiated into the African Lodge in 1809. In 1811 he was its Secretary. He was received both socially and fraternally in England, being a man of remarkable attainments and versatility. Later he became a member of the African Lodge of Philadelphia.

He was the founder of, and an active member of, the Belles Lettres Society, a literary group of young white men of Boston. He won the friendship and esteem of men like William Ellery Channing and William S. Shaw. Going to England about 1812 or 1813, he met Wilberforce, who sent him to Haiti at the request of the celebrated Emperor Christophe to organize an educational system for Haiti on the Lancastrian plan. In 1816 he introduced vaccination into the Island. Christophe made him a special envoy to England, where he was received with honor in the best social circles. While in England in 1816, he published *Haitian Papers*, in which he translated and made a commentary on the laws of Haiti. This same work appeared in an American edition in 1818. Because of some differences, and possibly excessive use of an envoy's authority, he was recalled by Christophe but prudently came to Philadelphia instead of returning to Haiti. In Philadelphia he was a lay reader in St. Thomas Episcopal Church founded by Absalom Jones, and also took an active part in anti-slavery conventions. Christophe was overthrown in 1820 and Saunders returned to Haiti, where he was made Attorney General by President Boyer. He died at Port Au Prince in 1839. (12)

Richard Allen was the founder and first Bishop of the African Methodist Episcopal Church. He was born a slave in Philadelphia and was sold to a farmer in Dover, Delaware. He became a religious worker and was converted by Methodists. They permitted him to conduct services at home, where he converted his master, who later freed Allen and his family. Allen studied privately and preached to Negroes and Whites. He traveled throughout Delaware, New Jersey, Pennsylvania, and Maryland. In 1784, at the first general conference of the Methodist Church in Baltimore, he was accepted by the hierarchy as a minister of promise. He returned to Philadelphia in 1786 and was asked to preach occasionally. He began conducting prayer meetings among Negroes and sought to establish a separate place of worship. Both Negroes and Whites objected. He attracted large numbers of Negroes to the church where he preached, but Whites objected to their presence and pulled them from their knees one Sunday, ordering them to the gallery. Rather than submit to the insult, the Negroes withdrew and established in 1787 an independent organization, The Free African Society. Some broke away to establish the Independent Bethel Church.

Allen was ordained a Deacon in 1799 and an Elder in 1816. There were 16 congregations by 1816, when he was chosen Bishop of the African Methodist Episcopal Church. (13)

"While Allen belonged to a particular religious denomination and was honored by it, he was more than the leader of a restricted religious group. He might be compared with the great reformers of history, but he was more comprehensive in his life and thought than these men. He was a religious leader because he lived in an age when religion was dominant in the life of his people, but he was also a leader in the other avenues of life. He led the way in economic and social life and organization for the people who looked to him for leadership in these aspects of life."

"Richard Allen regarded the Negro people as an oppressed minority who needed an aggressive leadership in order to achieve its emancipation. He did not understand that the exploitation of Black men and women was an economic phenomenon and that it would not be overcome without economic reorganization. Misguided as he was in this respect, he began his work for freedom in the first of the economic organizations in Negro Life—The Free African Society. He was soon led to begin a religious organization but he was ever mindful of the social aspects of his movement, and not once did he seem to lose sight of this. He was no narrow religionist, although at times he showed that he was superstitious and mystical, as were most of the earlier Negro leaders. He saw clearly that the exploiters of the masses could keep them in subjugation only as they desired to submit to their overlords. He saw that the struggle for human rights, so far as the Negroes were concerned, must be waged partly from within the group itself. He saw also that there were allies in other racial minorities upon whom he could depend. He would find these allies, and with their assistance he would begin a movement from within the submerged people to end the exploitation of Black Americans by White Americans." (14)

In his Diary, William Bentley D.D., Pastor of the East Church of Salem, Massachusetts, wrote on September 20, 1807 (page 321, vol. 3) "Prince Hall, the leading African of Boston & author of several Masonic addresses, tells me that an African preacher was in Boston who had been ordained by Bishop White of Philadelphia in the English Forms."

Prince Hall was referring to *Absalom Jones*, the first Grand Master of the Prince Hall Grand Lodge of Pennsylvania.

After passing an examination for Holy Orders, the knowledge of Greek and Latin being waived in his case, Absalom Jones was ordained a reader of divine service and a Deacon by Bishop White in August, 1795 and was reported by Bishop White as a priest in 1804. (15)

Absalom Jones was born in Sussex, Delaware, on November 6, 1746. He learned to read while a slave, and by saving his extra money he was able to purchase a speller, a Testament, and other books. He was brought to Philadelphia by his master, who opened a store there in 1762. The work of Absalom Jones was "to store, pack up and carry out goods." Through the assistance of the store's clerk he learned to write, and in 1766 he began to attend night school. Through the assistance of a friend, he succeeded in purchasing the freedom of his wife, who he married while a slave in 1770. He purchased a home with his savings and finally secured his own freedom by purchase in 1784. Jones continued in the service of his former master, working for wages. He purchsed a plot of ground and built two houses on it from which he received rentals. By 1787 he was regarded as one of the substantial colored citizens in Philadelphia and as a leader among the colored members of St. George's Methodist Episcopal Church. (16)

Jones was the first Master of the African Lodge of Pennsylvania, the first Grand Master of that Grand Lodge and the first ordained colored Episcopal priest in America. (17)

At fourteen, James Forten sailed with Stephen Decatur aboard the *Royal Louis* as a powderboy during the Revolutionary War. When he was captured and offered a chance to go to England, the boy answered, *"I am here a prisoner for the liberties of my country, I never, never, shall prove a traitor to her interests."* (18) He later invented a device that aided in the control of sails and became a millionaire (actually he made about $100,000) and built a sail factory employing fifty Negro and White workers. Forten used the money his invention earned to further the abolitionist cause. He contributed a considerable sum to William Lloyd Garrison's *Liberator* during the first crucial years of its publication and was an important influence on the White editor. Forten became President of Philadelphia's Moral Reform Society, won a citation for saving a number of people from drowning, and helped recruit 2,500 Negroes to defend his city during the War of 1812. (19) Like Marrant, Saunders, Forten and Jones were Prince Hall Freemasons and acquainted with Prince Hall.

On June 24, 1789, Brother Marrant, Chaplain of The African Lodge, in celebration of the festival of St. John the Baptist, delivered his memorable sermon to the Lodge. It was a discourse studded with passages of such uncommon beauty and power, one wonders how and when this self-taught wanderer ever mastered the eloquence that suffuses it. A jeremiad aimed against the "monsters" of White racism, it summons its hearers to a new sense of Black worth and dignity.

"Man is a wonderful creature, and not undeservedly said to be a little world, a world within himself, and containing whatever is found in the Creator. In him is the spiritual and immaterial nature of God, the reasonableness of Angels, the sensitive power of brutes, the vegetative life of planets, and the virtue of all the elements he holds converse within both worlds. Thus man is crowned with glory and honour; he is the most remarkable workmanship of God. And is man such a noble creature and made to converse with his fellow men that are of his own order, to maintain mutual love and society, and to serve God in consort with each other? Then what can these God-provoking wretches think, who despise their fellow men, as tho' they were not of the same species with themselves, and would if in their power deprive them of the blessings and comforts of this life, which God in his bountiful goodness, hath freely given all his creatures to improve and enjoy? Surely such monsters never came out of the hand of God... ."

To his Black brethren, he counsels a just pride in their African forbears—"Tertullian, Cyprian, Origen, Augustine, Chrysotom... and many others." There are some, he tells them, who "despise those they would make, if they could, a species below them, and as not made of the same clay with themselves"; "but if you study the holy book of God, you will there find that you stand on the level not only with them, but with the greatest kings on the earth, as Men and as Masons... ."

The accomplishments of these brethren illustrate graphically one theme that will recur within this work, that the history of Prince Hall Freemasonry is the history of the Black man in America.

A

S E R M O N

PREACHED on the 24th DAY of JUNE 1789,

BEING THE FESTIVAL

OF

St. JOHN the Baptist,

AT THE REQUEST

OF THE

RIGHT WORSHIPFUL THE GRAND MASTER

PRINCE HALL,

AND

THE REST OF THE BRETHREN

OF THE

AFRICAN LODGE

OF THE

HONORABLE SOCIETY

OF

FREE and ACCEPTED MASONS

IN BOSTON.

By the Reverend Brother MARRANT,
CHAPLAIN.

Job xxxii. 17 ver. I said, I will answer also my part, I also
will shew mine opinion. ——

BOSTON
PRINTED AND SOLD AT THE BIBLE AND HEART.

A Sermon

REFERENCE FOR PART III

1. William H. Upton, Transactions of the Quatuor Coronati Lodge No. 2076, Vol. XIII, January 1900, *"Prince Hall Letter Book"* London, p. 54.
2. Selina, Countess of Huntingdon, born 1707, died 1791, was head of a sect of Calvinistic Methodists who became known as "The Countess of Huntingdon's Connections."
3. Upton, *op. cit.*, p. 5.
4. Sidney Kaplan, *The Black Presence in the Era of The American Revolution 1770-1800* (Washington, D.C., National Portrait Gallery, Smithsonian Institution, 1973) p. 97.
5. John Marrant, Sermon (Reprinted for private circulation, edited by Arthur A. Schomburg, Past Grand Secretary, M.W. Prince Hall Grand Lodge of New York, New Yor, 1920, (author's collection) cited by the *Journal of Negro History*, Vol. 21, 1936, p. 394-395.
6. Rev. William Aldridge, *A Narrative of the Lord's Wonderful Dealings with John Marrant, A Black* (now going to preach the Gospel in Nova Scotia) etc., London, 1785, 4th Edition, p. 40, cited in Journal of Negro History, Vol. 21, 1936, p. 395.
7. *Ibid*, p. 397.
8. Lemuel Haynes enlisted as a Minuteman. A Connecticut Negro, he served at Lexington and with the Ticonderoga Expedition. He later became a member of the Green Mountain Boys of Vermont and took part in the capture of Fort Ticonderoga. In 1785 he became a pastor of a White congregation in Torrington, Connecticut. He was the first Negro Congregational pastor. He later became pastor of a White Congregational church in Manchester, N.H. Peter M. Bergman, *The Chronological History of the Negro in America*, New York: Harper & Row, 1969, p. 49, 51, 62 and 110.
9. Kaplan, *op. cit.*, p. 99.
10. Harry E. Davis, *A History of Freemasonry Among Negroes in America*, United Supreme Council, A.A.S.R., Northern Jurisdiction, U.S.A., Prince Hall Affiliation, Inc., 1946, p. 268-9.
11. *The Autobiography of William Bentley Fowle* Ms. with Massachusetts Historical Society, cited by Harry E. Davis, *Ibid*, p. 267.
12. *Ibid*, p. 42.
13. *Dictionary of American Biography*, Vol. XVI, p. 382, cited by Davis, *Ibid*, p. 41, 291-293.
14. Peter M. Bergman, *The Chronological History of the Negro in America, Ibid*, p. 41.
15. Charles H. Wesley, *Richard Allen—Apostle of Freedom*, Washington, D.C.: The Associated Publishers, Inc., 1935, p. viii.
16. *Ibid*, p. 73.
17. *Ibid*, p. 59.
18. Davis, *op. cit.*, p. 291.
19. William Loren Katz, *Eyewitness, The Negro In American History*, New York: Pitman Publishing Corporation, 1971, p. 47.

IV

PRINCE HALL MASONRY AND THE CIVIL WAR

In the beginning of the Civil War, it was made quite clear that President Lincoln was very reluctant to use Negroes in the armed services and that the War Department had no intentions of using Negroes as soldiers. (1)

But by the close of 1862, the military situation was very discouraging. The Union troops had been beaten at Fredericksburg and Vicksburg, and Lincoln was forced to reverse his stand. He issued his long awaited Emancipation Proclamation on January 1, 1863 (2). And even in this, Lincoln indicated little enthusiasm for the widespread use of Negro soldiers. The proclamation merely stated that Blacks would be used only for garrison duty and to man ships. (3)

John Albion Andrew was inaugurated Governor of the Commonwealth of Massachusetts on the fifth of January, 1861. He had long been a zealous abolitionist and was a personal friend of Lewis Hayden, then Grand Master of the Prince Hall Grand Lodge of Massachusetts. Hayden, a powerful leader among the Black community of Boston, had first suggested to Andrew that he run for the office of Governor. (4)

In 1862, events were taking shape that would play a major role not only in the history of the nation but in Prince Hall Masonry as well. Governor Andrew visited Grand Master Hayden's residence at 66 Philips Street as he often did, for Thanksgiving dinner, a gesture which must have been viewed by the Black community as a strong sign of friendship between these two leaders, one White and one Black—a friendship which was remarkable, considering the times.

Grand Master Hayden was without a doubt a most remarkable individual. He was the first Grand Secretary of the Prince Hall Grand Lodge of New York and a leader of the Boston Vigilance Committee whose very house was a station of the Underground Railroad. (5) It was at Hayden's house that the abolitionist John Brown stayed during one of his last trips to Boston. (6) Hayden was also a Masonic scholar and the author of several Masonic works: *Caste Among Masons* (1886), *Grand Lodge Jurisdictional Claim or War of Races* (1868), and *Masonry Among Colored Men in Massachusetts* (1871).

At friendly get-togethers with the Governor at the Hayden home, the Grand Master put John Andrew in touch with many prominent Prince Hall Masons from New York, Pennsylvania, Ohio and Rhode Island as well as Massachusetts. (7)

In 1863, the Governor, armed with authority from the Secretary of War, began to seek Black volunteers to fill the 54th Regiment of that State. This unit became the first all-Black regiment from the North. Realizing that the Black population of Massachusetts was too small to fill the necessary quota, Governor Andrew selected as recruiting agents the most well-known Negroes of the day to assist in the project. Among the brethren of the Craft who aided the plan by speeches or as agents was Bro. Martin R. Delany. (8) Bro. Delany was a Past Master of St. Cyprian Lodge No. 13 of Pittsburgh, Pennsylvania and a District Deputy of the Western District for the National Grand Lodge. (9) He had the distinction, one among many, of writing the first printed work on Negro Freemasonry in the United States, *The Origin and Objects of Freemasonry, Its Introduction into the United States and Legitimacy among Colored Men.* Delany later became the first Black Major in the United States Army, appointed to this rank by President Lincoln. He was, among other things, a Black Nationalist and co-authored *Search for a Place—Black Separatism and Africa, 1860* which deals with Black resettlement in Africa as the solution to the problems of slavery and discrimination. Delany was also a dynamic orator. Oratory was one form that Black Americans used to assert their worth and to validate their claim to human rights. It was this form that helped demolish the myth of the natural inferiority of Blacks, and in oratory Delany was a Past Master. He was without a doubt one of the most outstanding figures in Black history. Though very much misunderstood, he saw the war as a means for the slaves to escape their bondage and return back to Mother Africa. Delany had little respect for the Caucasian race and little liking for America. Unlike Grand Master Hayden, Delany had never been a slave.

Also aiding Governor Andrew was John Mercer Langston, a Prince Hall Freemason. His father, Charles M. Langston, was one of the organizers and the first Worshipful Master of St. Mark's Lodge No. 7,

Columbus, Ohio. (10) Both gave assistance to David Jenkins, later the 17th Grand Master of the Prince Hall Grand Lodge of Ohio, in the Underground Railroad movement. (11) Bro. John Langston became Inspector General of the Freedmen's Bureau, a Congressman elected to the House of Representatives, and author of *Freedom and Citizenship* (1883) which was a collection of his speeches and *From the Virginia Plantation to the National Capitol* (1894).

William Schouler, Adjutant-General of Massachusetts, states "Lewis Hayden, formerly a slave in Kentucky but who had been for many years employed in the office of the Secretary of State, entered warmly into the business of recruiting colored soldiers for Massachusetts and visited Pennsylvania and other states to advance that interest." (12)

Though one cannot draw any definitive conclusions from this statement, it opens that door to several possibilities. Grand Master Hayden, who was traveling to these several states for Governor Andrew, may have also been making official visits to these areas as a leader of the Underground Railroad as well as Grand Master of Massachusetts, since many of the Prince Hall Masonic lodge halls, as well as the homes of individual members, were stations for the Underground Railroad.

In a letter to him while he was in Pennsylvania, Governor Andrew wrote, "I do not wish to be understood to favor it. But if, by work in Pennsylvania, you can help those fleeing from slavery through that state to reach Massachusetts, where they will be received into all the rights and advantages of our own citizens, I shall be glad. I do not want either to speculate out of the blood or courage of colored men, but I rejoice in having been instrumental in giving them a chance to vindicate their manhood, and to strike a telling blow for their own race, and [for] the freedom of all their posterity. Every race has fought for liberty, and its own progress. The colored race will create its own future, by its own brain, hearts, and hands. If Southern slavery should fall by the crushing of the Rebellion, and colored men have no hand, and play no conspicuous part, in the task, the result would leave the colored man a mere helot; the freedman, a poor, despised, subordinate body of human beings, neither strangers nor citizens, but 'contrabands,' who had lost their masters, but not found a country. All the prejudices, jealousies and political wishes of narrow ignorant men and demagogues would have full force and the black man would be a helpless victim of a policy which would give him no

peace short of his own banishment. The day that made a colored man
a soldier of the Union, made him a power in the land. It admitted him
to all the future of glory, and to all the advantages of an honorable
fame, which pertained to men who belonged to the category of
heroes. No one can ever deny the rights of citizenship in a country to
those who have helped to create it or to save it." (13)

There have been many speculations as to the presence of a Prince
Hall Military Lodge during the Civil War. (14) In most cases the
Masonic historians and writers have been wrong in their selection of
the military unit to which the Lodge was actually attached. The first
Prince Hall Masonic lodge attached to any military unit was assigned
to the 54th Massachusetts Volunteer Infantry.

Captain Luis F. Emilio, a Caucasian officer serving with this unit
writes, "First Sargeant Gray of Company C had received a Masonic
charter and organized a Lodge on Morris Island. The meeting place
was a dry spot in the marsh near our camp, where boards were set up
to shelter the members." (15) This was truly an historical milestone
for Prince Hall Freemasonry.

There is an air of mystery concerning the early Black Military
Masonic Lodge because only a handful of Black writers have written
the history of these early Black units, leaving it mostly in the hands of
their White officers or the manuscripts have yet to be discovered.
George Williams (16) and Joseph T. Wilson are the exception to the
rule. Both were outstanding historians, but even in their works there
is no mention of any Black Military Masonic Lodge.

What adds to the mystery is that all attempts to learn the identity of
this first military lodge and who actually authorized it has been a difficult but not impossible task. By exploring bits and pieces of
evidence, though not proven conclusively, the identity can be nar-
rowed down.

When one considers that during this time in the Black man's struggle for freedom from the bondage of slavery, and realizes that a handful of Prince Hall Freemasons would be meeting and practicing the
"Royal Art" within the line of the Union Army while fighting to make
their race free surely he must be impressed not only by the historical
significance but by the heroic aspects of their activities as well.

First Sargeant William H. Gray, who Captain Emilo states was the
organizer or Worshipful Master, was 38 years old and married, and
his occupation is listed on the rolls of the unit as seaman. He enlisted
at New Bedford, Massachusetts on February 14, 1863, and was

mustered out on August 20, 1865, receiving $50 for his service. His military record shows that on September 22, 1863, Sergeant Gray was on furlough and received $3.50 for transportation from New York to New Bedford, Massachusetts, from the Quartermaster Office. (17) It was during this trip which was the only furlough or leave of absence he had during his entire military service, that in all probability Sergeant Gray picked up the Charter of this Lodge from the Prince Hall Grand Lodge of Massachusetts.

Lewis Hayden in his address before the Prince Hall Grand Lodge of Massachusetts, December 27, 1865, St. John's Day, and three months after the 54th was mustered out of service, stated "It was the spirit of love to God and man that caused the Grand Lodge to establish a Lodge in South Carolina, and that at Charleston, S.C., has been duly warranted and constituted under the name of Hayden's Lodge No. 8."(18)

There is also Grand Master Hayden's petition for recognition submitted to the Caucasian Grand Lodge of Massachusetts in 1868 with the following: "Hayden Lodge No. 8, Charleston, S.C., withdrawn October 1868, and with other Lodges formed a Grand Lodge for the State of South Carolina." (19)

The actual formation of the Prince Hall Grand Lodge of South Carolina is not clear. Harry A. Williamson, the noted Prince Hall historian wrote, "Sometime during the early portion of the year 1867, the New Jersey Jurisdiction established Hayden Lodge at Charleston." (2) This statement was, of course, incorrect. William H. Grimshaw wrote that the Grand Lodge of Massachusetts established a Lodge in Charleston, S.C. (21) In a pamphlet written by J.N. Conna it is recorded that South Carolina was "instituted in 1869 by Lodges holding warrants from the National Grand Lodge." (22) South Carolina itself records in the Prince Hall Masonic Yearbook of 1968 only "that the Grand Lodge was organized by an Act of the General Assembly of South Carolina and approved on the 9th day of March 1872." Yet in the Committee on Foreign Correspondence for the Prince Hall Grand Lodge of Missouri for the Masonic year ending July 4, 1870, it is reported on page 30 under the heading "South Carolina": "This Grand Lodge has not been constituted a year, yet it was organized under favorble circumstances, and will make a strong body and addition to our ranks. M.W. Bro. Geo. E. Johnson, Grand Master. Address, Box 317, Charleston, S.C." The proceedings of Missouri for 1871, state "This vigorous young Grand Lodge enters her

Quartermaster's Office,

New-York, _Sept 11_ 1863.

Sir,

Transportation has been furnished to

W H H Gray a _Sergt_ of your

Company, on Furlough, from _Pence_ to

New Bedford Mass at an expense of $ _3 52_

which has been noted on his Furlough, and should be charged against

him on your next Muster Roll for Stoppage from his Pay.

I am, Sir,

Very respectfully,

Your ob'dt Serv't,

D Hnsn

Assistant Quartermaster.

Officer Commanding

Company _C_

_54_ Regiment _Mass_

_J.R._

Copy of Quartermaster's report showing date when Worshipful Master Gray, while on furlough, was able to pick up charter for Military Lodge.

second year under a fair sea..." and report that this Grand Lodge had six subordinate lodges.

Therefore, the claim by the Prince Hall Grand Lodge of South Carolina, that it was organized in 1872 is not correct. It is the writer's intention to show that this military Lodge attached to the 54th Massachusetts in 1863 was re-warranted in 1865, when the 54th left Charleston to be mustered out in August, and became one of the founding lodges that organized the current Prince Hall Grand Lodge of South Carolina!

Captain Emilio in his history of the 54th Massachusetts Volunteer Infantry records that "In Charleston the Masonic Lodge organized on Morris Lodge, of which Sergeant Gray of Company C was the Master, met in the third story of a house just across from the Citadel. Sergeants Vogelsang, Alexander Johnson, and Hemingway were among the members, who numbered some twenty-five or thirty. It is thought that the Charter of this Lodge was surrendered ultimately to Prince Hall Lodge of Boston whence it came." (23)

Of the names mentioed by Captain Emilio, we find that there were two Alexander Johnsons listed on the roster of the 54th. One, though, was only 16 years of age, so it is very doubtful that he was the person mentioned. The other was a Private from Company F. He was 34 years old, single, with an occupation listed as laborer. His home was Elmira, New York, and he enlisted on the 8th of April 1863. (24)

Also from Company F was Sergeant A.F. Hemingway, 28 years old, married, occupation listed as a barber. His home was Worcester, Massachusetts. (25)

Of the Masonic brethren named, one of the most intriguing is Sergeant, later First Lieutenant, Peter Vogelsang, a Quartermaster officer. His date of birth was August 21,1815, and his home was New York. He entered service in Brooklyn, New York, and was assigned to Company H on April 17, 1863, as a Quartermaster Sergeant. He was promoted to Second Lieutenant on April 28; then a few weeks later he was promoted to First Lieutenant on June 20, 1863. According to the roster, he was wounded on July 16, 1863, at James Island, South Carolina, and died April 4, 1887, in New York. (26)

What is of interest concerning Bro. Vogelsang is the fact that his name is mentioned in a number of books. In Bro. Charles H. Wesley's *Richard Allen—Apostle of Freedom*, (27) he is mentioned as having signed a circular in 1830 for the African Methodist Episcopal Church which was founded by another Prince Hall Mason, Bro. Richard

Bro. (Lt.) Peter Vogelsang Member of the First Prince Hall Masonic Military Lodge

CASUALTY SHEET.

Name, *Peter Vogelsang*

Rank, *Sergeant*, Company *H*, Regiment, *54*

Arm, *Inf.*, State,

Place of casualty, *James Island S.C.*

Nature of casualty, *Wounded*

Date of casualty, *July 16" 1863.*

FROM WHAT SOURCE THIS INFORMATION WAS OBTAINED.

Report of Killed, Wounded, and Missing of the *54* Regiment.
Brigade, *1* Division *10 & 18* Corps, dated

(Sgd) *Alfred H. Terry*
Brig. Genl. Comdg 1' Div.

And 16 & 9 2)

Thos Broderick

Clerk

Copy of casualty sheet on the wounding of Bro. Peter Vogelsang, member of
The Prince Hall Military Lodge.

Allen. His name is also mentioned in Benjamin Quarles' *Black Aboli-tionists* as having been a member of the Phoenix Society, a Negro self-improvement organization founded in New York in 1833. He was also a member of the Committee for Superintending the Application for Funds for the College for Colored Youth. (28) What is equally intri-guing is the fact that Vogelsang is also mentioned in the book *The Life and Public Service of Martin R. Delany,* in which Bro. Delany ex-claimed, "Brave Vogelsang, the intrepid lennox (sic)." (29) This brings us back to Martin R. Delany. He was by far one of the most dynamic individuals of his time as he lived so many adventures and each is a story within itself. As mentioned earlier, he was a Prince Hall Freemason with many accomplishments. (30) He was the first Black to achieve the rank of Major in the service of the United States Army, appointed to this rank from civilian life with the approval of President Lincoln and by the direction of the Secretary of War. He was mustered into service February 27, 1865, as Major, United States Col-ored Troops on detached services to the Freedman Bureau in South Carolina. (31)

And it is here that the Masonic lines may have crossed, with the Lodge attached to the 54th. The mere mention of Delany's words of "Brave Vogelsang" raises the speculation that the two may have been associated Masonically.

While at St. Helena Island, Delany was accused of "calculating to do harm, by inciting the colored people to deeds of violence," by the advice that he was giving to the ex-slaves to stand up for full freedom and resist re-enslavement by arms if necessary. This frightened the Whites who were present.

Delany's speech follows as it was reported in a letter from Lieuten-ant Edward M. Stoeber:

Headquarters, Assistant Commissioner
Bureau Refugees, Freedmen and Abandoned Lands
South Carolina, Georgia and Florida
Beaufort, S.C., July 24th, 1865

Br(eve)t Maj. S. M. Taylor
   Asst. Adjt Gen'l.
Major:

In obedience to your request, I proceeded to St. Helena Island, yesterday morning, for the purpose of listening to the public delivery of a lecture by Major Delany 104th Ne(gro) S.C. Troops.

I was accompanied by Lieut. A. Whyte jr 128th Ne(gro) S.C. Troops, under Col. C.H. Howard 128th Ne(gro) S.C. Troops, Com(an)d'g Post.

The meeting was held near "Brick Church," the congregation numbering from 500 to 600.

As introduction Maj. Delany made them acquainted with the fact, that slavery is absolutely abolished, throwing thunders of damnations and maledictions on all the former slave owners and people of the South, and almost condemned their souls to hell.

He says "it was only a war policy of the Government, to declare the slaves of the South free, knowing that the whole power of the South, laid in the possession of the slaves. But I want you to understand, that we would not have become free, had we not armed ourselves and fought out our independence" (this he repeated twice). He further says, "if I had been a slave, I would have been most troublesome and not to be conquered by any threat or punishment. I would not have worked, and no one would have dared to come near me. I would have struggled for life or death, and would have thrown fire and sword between them.

"I know you have been good, only too good. I was told by a friend of mine that when owned by a man and put to work on the field, he laid quietly down, and just looked out for the overseer to come along, when he pretended to work very hard. But he confessed to me, that he never had done a fair day's work for his master. And so he was right, so I would have done the same, and all of you ought to have done the same.

"People say that you are too lazy to work, that you have no intelligence to get on for yourself, without being guided and driven to the work by overseers. I say it is a lie, and a blasphemous lie, and I will prove it to be so.

"I am going to tell you now, what you are worth. As you know Christopher Columbus landed here in 1492. They came here only for the purpose to dig gold, gather precious pearls, diamonds and all sorts of jewels, only for the proud Aristocracy of the White Spaniards and Portuguese, to adorn their persons, to have brooches for their breasts, earrings for their ears, bracelets for their ankles and rings for their limbs and fingers. They found here (red men) Indians whom they obliged to dig and work and slave for them—but they found out that they died away too fast and cannot stand the work. In course of time they had taken some blacks (Africans) along with them and put them to work—they could stand it—and yet the Whites say they are superior to our race, though they could not stand it. (At the present day in some of the Eastern parts of Spain, the Spaniards there (having been once conquered by the black race) have black eyes, black hair, black complexion. They have Negro blood in them!!) The work was so profitable which those poor blacks did, that in the year 1502 Charles the V. gave permission to import into America yearly 4,000 blacks. The profit of these sales was so immense, that afterwards even the Virgin Queen of England and James the II, took part in the Slave trade and were accumulating great wealth for the Treasury of the Government. And so you always have been the means of riches.

"I tell you I have been all over Africa (I was born there) and I tell you (as I told to the Geographical Faculty in London) that those people there, are a well driving class of cultivators, and I never saw or heard of one of our brethren there to travel without taking seeds with him as much as he can carry and to sow it wherever he goes to, or to exchange it with his brethren.

So you ought to further know, that all the spices, cotton, rice and coffee has only been brought over by you, from the land of our brothers.

Your masters who lived in opulence, kept you to hard work by some contemptible being called overseer—who chastised and beat you whenever he pleased—while your master lived in some Northern town or in Europe to squander away the wealth only your unrequited far labor He never earned a single Dollar in his life. You men and women, every one of you around me, made thousands and thousands of dollars for your master. Only you were the means for your masters to lead the idle and inglorious life, and to give his children the education, which he denied to you, for fear you may awake to conscience. If I look around me, I tell you all the houses on this Island and in Beaufort, they are all familiar to my eye, they are the same structures, which I have met with in Africa. They have all been made by the Negroes, you can see it by such exteriors.

"I tell you they (white men) cannot teach you anything, and they could not make them because they have not the brain to do it. (after a pause) At least I mean the Southern people; Oh the Yankees they are smart. Now tell me from all you have heard from me, are you not worth anything? Are you those men whom they think God only created as a curse and for a slave? Whom they do not consider their equals? As I said before the Yankees are smart; they are good ones and bad ones. The good ones if they are good they are very good, if they are bad, they are very bad. But the worst and most contemptible, and even worse than even your masters were, are those Yankees who hired themselves as *overseers*.

"Believe not in these School teachers, Emissaries, Ministers, and agents, because they never tell you the truth, and I particularly warn you against those Cotton Agents, who come honey mouthed unto you, their only intent being to make profit by your inexperience.

"If there is a man who comes to you, who will meddle with your affairs, send him to one of your more enlightend brothers, who shall ask him who he is, what business he seeks with you, etc.

"Believe none but those Agents who are sent out by Government, to enlighten and guide you. I am an officer in the service of the U.S. Government, and ordered to aid Gen'l Saxton, who has been only lately appointed Asst Comr for South Carolina. So is Gen'l Wild Asst Comr for Georgia.

"When Chief Justice Chase was down here to speak to you, some of those malicious and abominable New York papers derived from it that he only seeks to be elected by you as President. I have no such ambition, I let them have for a President a white or a black one. I don't care who it be—it may be who has a mind to. I shall not be intimidated whether by threats or imprisonment, and no power will keep me from telling you the truth. So I expressed myself even at Charleston, the hotbed of those scoundrels, your old master, without fear or reluctance.

"So I will come to the main purpose for which I have come to see you. As before the whole South depended upon you, now the *whole country* will depend upon you. I give you an advice how to get along. Get up a community and get all the lands you can—if you cannot get any singly.

"Grow as much vegtables, etc., as you want for your families; on the other part of the land you cultivate rice and cotton. Now for instance 1. acre will grow a crop of cotton of $90—now a land with 10 acres will bring $900 every year; if one cannot get the land all yourself, the community can, and so you can divide the profit. There is tobacco for instance (Virginia is the great place for tobacco). There are whole squares at Dublin and Liverpool named after some place of tobacco notoriety, so you can see of what enormous value your labor was to the benefits of your masters. Now you understand that I want you to be the producers of this country. It is the wish of the Government for you to be so. We will send friends to you, who will further instruct you how to come to the end of your wishes. You see that by so adhereing to our views, you will become a wealthy and powerful population.

"Now I look around me and notice a man, barefooted, covered with rags and dirt. Now I ask, what is that man doing, for whom is he working. I hear that he works for that and that farmer for 30 cents a day. I tell you that must not be. That would be cursed slavery over again. I will not have it, the Government will not have it, and the Government shall hear about it. I will tell the Government. I tell you slavery is over, and shall never return again. We have now 200,000 of our men, well drilled in arms and used to warfare and I tell you it is with you and them that slavery shall not come back again, if you are determined it will not return again.

"Now go to work, and in a short time I will see you again, and other friends will come to show you how to begin. Have your fields in good order and well tilled and planted, and when I pass the fields and see a land well planted and well cared for, then I may be sure from the look of it, that it belongs to a free Negro, and when I see a field thinly planted and little cared for, then I may think it belongs to some man who works it with slaves. The Government decided that you shall have one third of the produce of the crops, from your employer, so if he makes $3.00 you will have to get $1. out of it for your labor.

"The other day some plantation owners in Virginia and Maryland offered $5. a month for your labour, but it was indignantly rejected by Gen'l Howard, the Commissioner for the Government."

These are the expressions, as far as I can remember, without having made notes at the time.

The excitement with the congregation was immense, groups were formed talking over what they have heard, and ever and anon cheers were given to some particular sentence of the speech.

I afterwards mingled with several groups, to hear their opinions. Some used violent language, "saying they would get rid of the Yankee employer." "That is the only man who ever told them the truth." "That now those men have to work themselves or starve or leave the country, we will not work for them anymore."

Some Whites were present, and listened with horror depicted in their faces to the whole performance. Some said, "What shall become of us now?" And if such a speech should be again given to those men, there will be open rebellion.

Major Delany was afterwards corrected by Mr. Town the Superintendent at that place, to the effect, that the pay of labourers on this Island is not 30 cents a day, but 30 cents a task, and that a man can easily make from 75 to 90 cents a day. Major Delany then corrected himself accordingly, saying that he must have been misinformed.

My opinion of the whole affair is that Major Delany is a thorough hater of the White race and excites the colored people unnecessarily. He even tried to injure the magnanimous conduct of the Government towards them, either intentionally or through want of knowledge.

He tells them to remember "that they would not have become free, had they not armed themselves and fought for their independence." This is a falsehood and a misrepresentation.

Our President Abraham Lincoln declared the colored men free before they were armed or armed or arming colored men. That individually individual in real bad feelings against the Government.

By giving them some historical facts and telling them that neither Indians nor Whites could stand the work, in this contry, he wants to impress them (the Colored men) with the idea that he in fact is not only superior, in a physical view, but also in intelligence. He says, "believe none of those ministers, schoolteachers, Emmisaries, because they never tell you the truth." It is only to bring distrust against all, and gives them to understand that they shall believe men of their own race. He openly acts and speaks contrary to the policy of the Government, advising them not to work for any man, but for themselves.

The intention of our Government, that all the men should be employed by their former masters, as far as possible, and contracts made between as superintended by some Officers empowered by the Government.

He says it would be slavery all over again. If a man should work for an employer, and that it must not be. Does he not give a hint of what they should do by his utterings "that if he had been a slave," etc.? Or by giving narrative of the slave who did not work for his master? Further as he says: "that a field should show by its appearance by whom and for whom it is worked."

The mention of having two hundred thousand men well drilled in arms; does he not hint to them what to do? If they should be compelled to work for employers?

In my opinion of this discourse, he was trying to encourage them to break the peace of society and force their way by insurrection to a position he is ambitious they should attain to.

    I am Major
    Very Respectfully
    Your Obedient Servant
    (sgd) Edward M. Stoeber
    1st Leut. 104th U.S.C.T.

A true copy
(Sgd) Edward M. Stoeber
  1st Lieut. 104th U.S.C.T.

As mentioned, the Masonic lines may have crossed, as Delany stayed at a private residence in the neighborhood of the citadel (32), or close to where the lodge was meeting, and that he used non-commissioned officers from the 54th and 55th, to include his son, Private Tousaint L. Delany of the 54th as aids. (33) There is no way of actually knowing, but it is an interesting speculation.

There could not have been much concern from the Caucasian

branch of the order about Black men practicing the "royal art" of Masonry at the time, as Governor Andrew, a non-Mason, was making presentations to the Prince Hall Grand Lodge of Massachusetts. His letter of December 21, 1864 to his friend, Grand Master Lewis Hayden is of interest.

> I send you with this note, for presentation to the Prince Hall Grand Lodge a gavel, made from a piece of the whipping-post at Hampton, Va. The gentleman who sent it to me says "This post or tree stood directly in the rear of the court-house, and in front of the jail. While I was cutting it about twenty colored men and women bore testimony to me that it was the identical post or tree that they had been tied to and had their backs lacerated with the whip.

> I also place in your hands, for the same purpose, a rude boat of straw, made in the woods by a poor refugee from slavery, Jack Flowers, who after a protracted journey through the forest, tracked by blood-hounds, reached a stream, down which he floated past the rebel pickets, till he reached a point guarded by the Union Army, where he landed a free man. A copy of his narrative will be given you for presentation with this interesting relic. (The straw boat, here spoken of, attracted much attention at the State House; and the wonder was, how so frail a bark could float a man from slavery to freedom. The narrative of Jack Flowers was furnished the Governor by a gentleman of the name of Judd, and tells a terrible tale of the suffering and wrongs of this poor man. It is too long to quote entire(ly). He was a slave in South Carolina, and escaped by means of his straw boat through the rebel pickets and landed safely at Hilton Head. Jack says that he made several attempts to pass the rebel picket line, but failed. We now quote from his narrative:

> "So when I found it was no use to get over that way, I concluded to try another. Uncle lent me his axe and knife, and I cut a lot of brushes, and a tough oak tree for splints, and went to work in the woods, and made this basket. It took me two days to weave it, after the stuff was all ready; the pitch I got by cutting into a tree, and catching the gum, which I boiled in a kettle of my sister's. The old shutter came from Dr. Fuller's house. It was three miles to the water, and I carried the basket along on my head in the dark night, for fear of the pickets. It was so late in the night when I got all ready to start in the creek, that I did not get down to the coosa till day clear, so I landed on a little hammock close by the mouth of the creek, and hid the boat and myself for another day. But before nine o'clock the next night, I put out and paddled over to Port Royal, too glad to get away. The Yankee picket wasn't asleep, but challenged me before I got near the shore, and I told him right off, that I was a runaway nigger coming ashore for freedom. The Rebel picket heard me, and after I got up the bank he hailed across 'Yanks, who have you got?' Yankee say, 'One of your fellows.' 'What you going to do with him?' 'Don't know, what do you think best?' 'Cut him up for fishbait, he ain't good for nothing else!' (34)

> "I know of no place more fitting for the preservation of these memorials of the barbarous institution that is now tottering with its rapidly approaching fall, than the association of free colored citizens of Massachusetts over which you

preside. Some among you may be reminded by them of the suffering and bondage from which the hands of God has delivered you, while others, whose happier lot it has been to be born and reared as free men in a free state, as they look upon these things will thank Him that He has been graciously pleased that their lines should fall in more pleasant places; and to those who shall come after you let the sight of these things be a perpetual memorial of God's favor to their fathers, in delivering them from their oppressors, as well as the victorious power which will one day right every wrong and justify every manful, dutiful, and sincere effort in behalf of truth, honor, and humanity.

I am faithfully yours, etc.
John A. Andrews"(35)

The Prince Hall Grand Lodge answered:

Boston, Jan. 20, 1865

To His Excellency, John A. Andrew, Governor of the Commonwealth of Massachusetts.

Sir, at a communication of Prince Hall Grand Lodge, held on the 27th day of December last, your interesting letter, presenting a gavel made from a piece of the whipping-post torn down by the Union soldiers near the Courthouse at Hampton, Va., and the basket-boat in which the refugee-hero Jack Flowers made his escape from slavery, was read by M.W.D.G.M. Robert Morris.

The undersigned were charged with the pleasant duty of tendering you the sincere thanks of Prince Hall Grand Lodge for these valuable relics, and the kind and sympathizing expressions contained in your letter.

The fraternity of which we are members is one of the most excellent and time honored institutions existing among civilized men. The Charter under which we exist, as a Lodge, is one of the most ancient in our country. The principles of our Order are universal, and its duties and obligations imperative and absolute. Nevertheless, the pernicious influence of slavery has caused our white brethren to remove an "ancient landmark," to foster an unchristian and unmasonic caste which makes them forgetful of their great duties and obligations to us, which we, as brethren, can never fail to practice toward them; and for this Christian spirit which thus animates us, we devoutly thank the Great Architect of the Universe.

The possession of the boat affords us the liveliest pleasure and satisfaction. Hereafter, we shall call it our ark. We can well understand the feelings of Jack Flowers, when, after making his escape from slavery, pursued by cruel and savage men, accompanied by bloodhounds, scarcely less merciless than their masters, baffling the keen scent of the dogs, and the vigilance of the men, tired, worn, and weary, he sat down in the dense woods and constructed this rude and frail ark. Surely as the God of our fathers guided Moses as he led the children of Israel through the Red Sea to their promised Canaan, so was He with this poor fugitive, tenderly guiding him in his flight from slavery to freedom.

The manufacture of this gavel from a piece of that relic of barbarism, the old whipping post, a tool so Masonically significant, was a happy conception of your excellency. It will constantly remind us of the difference between obedience wrung from an oppressed race by power and might, with thumb-screws, whipping posts, branding irons, and the lash, and that obedience so willing rendered by us as freemen to those in authority, where the rights of the poor and most humble citizen are sacred and protected by law.

We avail ourselves of this opportunity to thank you for the disinterred and real friendship always manifested by you for our race; for your kind and sincere sympathy in our misfortunes; for your determined efforts in private and public life in favor of immediate emancipation, and in behalf of civil and political rights.

Especially do we thank you, as governor of our good old Commonwealth, for your noble and successful efforts in raising the Fifty-Fourth and Fifty-Fifth Regiments of Massachusetts Volunteers, the first two colored regiments sent into the service; thus setting an example to the other States, as patriotic as it has proved successful. Surely it must be a source of great happiness to your excellency to know that the conduct of these troops has been such as to force the general government to adopt your policy, and that today three hundred thousand colored soldiers are in the field fighting nobly for the salvation of the United States of America.

In behalf of Prince Hall Grand Lodge, and for ourselves, we are, very respectfully,
Your excellency's obliged and humble servants.

ROBERT MORRIS
THOMAS DALTON
FRANCIS P. CLARY (36)

There can be little doubt therefore of the fact that the Caucasian officers of the 54th were aware that this Prince Hall Masonic Military Lodge was attached to this unit. Many of these officers were members of the Fraternity, and as Captain Emilo points out, were purchasing Masonic emblems so they would insure themselves of a Masonic burial, in case of their deaths.(37)

Captain Emilo mentions that "...Dr. Albert G. Mackey, and other citizens appeared, and representing that the Rebel rear guard was still in place, begged protection and assistance in quelling the flames which threatened the total destruction of the city."(38)

Dr. Albert Gallatin Mackey, known throughout the Masonic world as author of *Jurisprudence of Freemasonry, Encyclopedia of Freemasonry* and a number of other valuable historical and judicial Masonic writings, was a collector for the Port of Charleston (39) and was, as the noted Prince Hall Masonic scholar Harry Williamson records, "quite unfavorable to the Freemasonry of the Negro."(40)

The first Black officer of the 54th, sister unit the 55th Massachusetts, was Chaplain John H. Bowles, who years later became the Grand Historian of the Prince Hall Grand Lodge of Ohio, Deputy Grand Master and Chairman of the Committee on Foreign Correspondence. There is a likelihood that members of both units comprised the Military lodge. (41)

In further support of this writer's theory that Hayden Lodge No. 8 of Charleston, South Carolina, was either this Miliary lodge attached to the 54th or evolved from it, is the fact that Grand Master Lewis Hayden had leveled a bitter attack on President Andrew Johnson before the Prince Hall Grand Lodge at the Festival of St. John the Evangelist, held December 27, 1865. In his speech he mentions his visit to Charleston:

"That at Charleston, S.C., has been duly warranted and constituted under the name of Hayden Lodge No. 8. Its master is Brother Robert S. Lord...I found in Charleston, S.C., a still higher class of people, even than at Petersburg, as regards the general education, the mechanical arts, and all the elements which tend to make a first class society. In proof of this, I have brought with me a list of applications for initiations to their Lodges, the signers of which will compare favorable with the members of any Masonic Lodge, either white or black, in the United States..."(42)

The second Prince Hall Military Masonic Lodge to serve during the Civil War was Phoenix Lodge No. 1, and its existence has been hinted at in a number of Masonic historical books.

Other than the African Lodge 459, there has been no other Prince Hall Lodge that has had its charter or warrant reproduced so many times by Masonic writers and historians attempting to show their knowledge of Prince Hall Masonic history. For the most part, their versions of its history were incorrect.

Historians, be they Masonic or otherwise, have an obligation to present, as nearly as is possible, factual material. Statements such as, "The charter (of Phoenix Lodge No. 1) states that it was granted by the 29th U.S. Colored Troops, but it is possible and probable the printer reversed the "9" and it should have been the 26th Colored Regiment sponsored by the Union League Club of New York"(43) are ridiculous. Such misstatements show the abuse and mistreatment that Prince Hall Freemasonry has had to suffer at the hands of those who have no business in attempting to write on a subject of which they have no knowledge.

On the other hand, those Prince Hall Freemasons who attempt to write the history of their Fraternity likewise have an obligation to write the facts and to verify those facts before they attempt to pass them on to the Craft as Masonic history.

Harry E. Davis, a well-meaning historian of Prince Hall Masonry, in his *Freemasonry Among Negroes, etc.,* states that "the 29th Regiment Connecticut Colored Troops were organized in Fair Haven in February 1864. It was a State Volunteer Organization but was frequently called a Federal Regiment, hence its identity is often confused."(44)

Nothing could be further from the truth. To set the record straight, the earliest recruit for the 29th Regiment Connecticut Colored Infantry (the correct designation of the unit) was enlisted August 11, 1863. Most of the men came to the regiment at its rendezvous in New Haven during the last three months of the year. The full number was attained January 1864. For lack of officers it was not mustered into the United States service until March 8, 1864. (45)

The warrant of Phoenix Lodge was issued under the authority of the Grand Lodge of New York (National Grand Lodge) and was signed by David Gordon as Grand Master and attested by Samuel J. Scottron, Grand Secretary, Pro. Tem.(46)

The warrant appointed Alexander (the warrant reads Alex) Herritage Newton as Worshipful Master. Bro. Newton was a Commissary Sergeant in Company E, and his date of enlistment was December 18, 1863.

The life of Bro. Newton was very impressive and inspiring. He was dedicated to the upbringing of his race, a devotion to his religion, and a love of Prince Hall Freemasonry. Though his parents had been slaves, he was "free" born in New Bern, on Craven Street, Craven County, North Carolina. He was an educated man with high intelligence and strong religious persuasion, who would author an autobiography and include a sketch of the 29th Regiment to which the second Prince Hall Lodge was attached.(47)

Bro. Newton wrote in the preface of this book: "I have named the book *Out of the Briars*, because the figure is a befitting one in my own life. Although free born, I was born under the curse of slavery, surrounded by the thorns and briars of prejudice, hatred, persecution, and the suffering incident of this fearful regime. I, indeed, came out of the briars, torn and bleeding. I came out of poverty and ignorance. I did not have any of the advantages of the schools. I learned what little I know by listening to the educated white people talk. I picked up a great deal in this way."(48)

In Newton's autobiography one can see the workings of Prince Hall Masonry and the influence of the African Methodist Episcopal

REGIMENTAL WARRANT.

To all whom it may concern:

WISDOM, STRENGTH AND BEAUTY.

I, *David Boyd*, Most Worshipful Grand Master for the State of New York and Masonic Jurisdiction thereunto belonging, and National Masonic Union.

Having received a petition from the members of the 29th United States Colored Troops, praying for a Charter, to empower them to meet as a Lodge of Free Masons in said Regiment, to work according to the ancient Constitution, laws, and usages of Freemasonry, according to the ancient York Rite, and they, the said members of the above named Regiment, having to my satisfaction been well recommended.

I do, by virtue of the power in me vested, grant this as their Lawful Warrant, so long as they, the said members, shall conform to all the laws and usages of the Order, empowering them to work in their Regiment and nowhere else, and in no manner whatever to interfere with the rights of any established Lodge or Grand Lodge.

Furthermore, I do appoint our worthy and beloved brother *Alex H. Newton* to be the Worshipful Master; *John Andrews*, Senior Warden, and *Richard Giles* Junior Warden of said Lodge, to be called and known by the name and title of

PHŒNIX LODGE NO. 1.

And I do furthermore authorize and empower our said worthy and beloved brethren, to admit and make Free Masons, according to the most ancient, and honorable custom of the royal craft, so long as the above named Regiment shall remain together as such, and not longer, and on the return of the Regiment, this warrant shall be deposited with the most worshipful Grand Master for the State of New York.

Now, Brethren, we do command you, and your successors in office, to make regular quarterly returns to the Grand Master of all work done, with your tax and assessments for the same.

Now, by the grace of God, I, *David Gordon* Most Worshipful Grand Master for the State of New York, and Masonic jurisdiction thereunto belonging, do, by the power and authority to me committed, sign this warrant and cause the great seal of the Most Worshipful Grand Lodge to be here affixed this *18th* day of *March* A.D. 1864, A.L. 5864.

Attest.

David Gordon M. W. G. M.

Samuel J. Scottron, R. W. G. S. *Pro Tem*

Warrant granted by "Compact Grand Lodge" of New York for a Negro Military Lodge during Civil War.

Church, both having played a major role in sustaining Black America during the dark, brutal days of slavery. On page after page the reader is introduced to such Prince Hall Freemasons as Paul Drayton (49), Dr. Peter W. Ray (50), John Milton Turner (51), William Paul Quinn (52), and others who played some role in the development of Bro. Newton. The autobiography gives no information on Phoenix Lodge during Bro. Newton's stay with the military unit however.

His military record states that he joined the 29th on March 8, 1864, ten days before the warrant was issued creating the Lodge; but his autobiography gives March 8 as the date the Regiment broke camp and left New Haven for Annapolis, Maryland.

The Regiment spent eight to ten days in Maryland, then departed for Hilton Head, South Carolina. Therefore, if the warrant was issued on March 18, it must have been received by Bro. Newton in South Carolina, and would be the second warrant dispatched to a Prince Hall Worshipful Master while on duty in this Southern State.

Bro. Newton was appointed a Sergeant October 31, 1864 and was mustered out October 24, 1865.

The Senior Warden as named in the warrant was Bro. John A. Andrews, a Private in Company D. Bro. Andrews was a resident of Fairfield. He enlisted December 16, 1863. He joined the 29th also on the 8th of March 1864 and, likewise, was mustered out October 24, 1865.

The Junior Warden as named in the warrant was Bro. Richard Giles, a Corporal of Company H. His residence was New Haven. The date of his enlistment was December 31, 1863. He joined the unit and was, likewise, mustered out on the same dates as the other officers of the Lodge.

The warrant of Phoenix Lodge, like all military charters, specified that it was restricted in its jurisdiction to the Regiment only. And it was commanded not to interfere in any manner with the rights of any established Lodge or Grand Lodge! The right to work as a Lodge was limited to the time the Regiment should remain together, as such, and not longer. It was further enjoined that when the Regiment was mustered out, the warrant was to be deposited with the Grand Master of New York. The warrant has distinction of being the only known charter of its kind warranted to a Prince Hall Military Lodge during the Civil War.(53)

Harry E. Davis rightfully records that the Regiment was disbanded in the latter part of 1865 after its final service on the Mexican border. It had arrived at Brazo de Santiago, Texas, July 3, 1865, and from there it had gone to Brownsville, Texas. The Regiment arrived back at Hartford, November 21 (Bro. Newton states October 24) and the next day the unit was paid and discharged. The 29th fought at Petersburg, Virginia, August 12 to September 21, 1864; Chapin's Farm, Virginia September 29, 1864; Richmond, Virginia, September 30 to October 1, 1864; Darby Town Road, Virginia, October 13, 1864, and Kell House, Virginia, October 27 and 28, 1864. The Regiment suffered 470 casualties.

The Worshipful Master, Bro. Newton, makes no mention of the Lodge in his autobiography, nor do the names Bro. Andrews, the Senior Warden, or Bro. Giles, the Junior Warden, appear. As a Commissary Sergeant, he would normally store his supplies in a house or under some shelter so these areas were probably where the Lodge was meeting.

Under the title *"Religious and Civic Pioneering Among the Craftsmen"* from the book, *Footprints of Prince Hall Masonry in New Jersey* (54) by P.G.M. Aldrage B. Cooper, a section is set aside for Bro. Newton, and it is herewith printed in its entirety. Though incorrect in some detail, it is interesting nevertheless.

ALEXANDER HERRITAGE NEWTON was born in New Bern, North Carolina in 1837. His father was a slave, but his mother was a free woman. Young Newton accompanied his family when they moved North and settled in New Haven, Connecticut where Newton volunteered for service in the 29th Regiment of United States Colored Troops. He served as Commissary Sergeant on the Non-Commissioned Staff of that Connecticut Volunteer Infantry, and won a promotion from a Sergeancy of Company E on October 24, 1865. This record is to be found in the office of the Adjutant General at Hartford, Connecticut.

While he was in the Regiment, Newton and his military associates were granted a warrant by the Compact Grand Lodge in New York, under the date of March 18, 1864, to open and hold a lodge under the title of Phoenix Lodge Number 1. Alexander Newton was named first Master of that Military Lodge, the only lodge of its kind known to have existed during the Civil War. [As shown, this statement is not correct.] In view of the date of dissolution of that Lodge, it is quite probable that Newton was the only Master of that Lodge. The Regiment in which he soldiered served on the Mexican Border, and when it was disbanded in the later part of 1865, the warrant was surrendered to the parent body in accordance with the terms under which it had been issued.

The Williamson Collection on Negro Masonry at the 136th Street Branch of the New York Public Library houses the original charter issued to Phoenix Lodge, and the author has had the pleasure of examining the document in the presence of the founder of the collection. [The author being P.G.M. Cooper and the

Rev. Alexander Herritage Newton, D.D.

Alexander H. Newton in Military Uniform, Commissary Sergeant
29th Regiment Connecticut Volunteers.

founder, Rev. Alexander Williamson] A full page photograph of the document appears in the Yearbook edition on Negro Masonry.

Where Newton received the degrees of Symbolic Masonry is not definitely known. He may have received them in a New York City Lodge affiliated with the Compact Grand Lodge in New York previous to his selection as Master of the Regimental Lodge, or in the Military Lodge, or even in Connecticut in a previously established Lodge, although the Grand Lodge of Connecticut was not formed until 1873.

After he had received his schooling in New York City, in Pennington Seminary in New Jersey, and [in] Lincoln University in Pennsylvania, Newton was admitted into the Ministry of the African Methodist Episcopal Church. In 1870 he was taken into the Philadelphia Conference of the Church. Later he was assigned to a Pulaki, Tennessee charge. He was ordained a Deacon at Nashville in 1873, and, as an Elder in the Church, he was transferred to Pine Bluff, Arkansas.

In turn, Newton was transferred to the Louisiana Conference [and] then to the North Carolina Conference, where he was stationed in Raleigh. In 1880, the well-traveled pastor finally came into the New Jersey Conference, where he was to remain, his first assignment being at Morristown. After Morristown, Newton moved to Trenton and Camden in succession. The edifice presently occupied by the Macedonia congregation was completed during Newton's pastorate.

Although it is probable and possible [sic] that Newton may have been associated with the Craft in Morristown and Trenton, the oldest record extant with his name list(s) him on the roll of Rising Sun Lodge, Number 1, Camden. At that time that Lodge had six Past Grand Masters of Masons in New Jersey on its register.

Early in the 1900's Newton was named Grand Chaplain, which office he held until his demise. As a member of Grand Lodge, R. W. Alexander H. Newton was the Representative of Grand Lodge of Colorado near New Jersey and for several years officiated as Chairman of the Committee on Charity and [of] the Committee on Memorials. In 1911 Newton introduced a resolution before the Grand Lodge which suggested a simple method of participation by every craftsman in the acquisition of a home for indigent Masons. But the proposition, after due consideration, was turned down.

Alexander Newton was a Royal Arch Mason and a Knight Templar, and in the latter body he held a position in the Grand Commandery. With another New Jersey Mason of renown, Newton was one of the incorporators of the Supreme Council, Ancient and Accepted Scottish Rite, N.M.J.; the date of the incorporation of the body being (sic) September 21, 1898, and the place of incorporation, Camden, New Jersey.

Brother Newton was an Active (33°) for New Jersey and a member of DeHugo Consistory, Number 2, in Camden. He held the office of Treasurer-General, H.E. from 1908 to 1917, and in the latter year he was named Grand Prior to the Supreme Council, serving the office until his death.

The middle name of Alexander Herritage Newton was selected for the name of the military Lodge that was instituted at Camp Kilmer, New Brunswick, on March 8, 1949.

Newton is described as a Christian man possessing Christian charity, and he was admired as a man of culture, and orator and a powerful preacher. After a fruitful sojourn on this earth, and at the age of eighty four, Newton retired on May 4, 1921, mourned and missed by his host of friends, his family and fellows craftsmen.

A late Grand Master of New York, M. W. Edward W. Parker in his address to his Grand Lodge on June 1, 1921, referred to the fact that Alexander Newton, in March of that year, had been present in Brooklyn attending the Easter Service of King David Consistory. Continuing, the speaker described Newton as a "splendid character and a Christian gentleman."

The following is taken from the resolution adopted by the New Jersey Grand Lodge, on December 27, 1921, at its Annual Communication:

"…we meet at this hour to pay tribute of love and respect to his memory…his counsels were wise because his knowledge was thorough. His friendship was sincere because his nature was free from guile and hypocrisy. His labors were unremitting because his love for the institution and its craftsmen was earnest and steadfast. His speech was direct because his heart was sincere and true. He loved life and his fellows. He ornamented and adorned the spheres in which he moved. He reaps in our abundant tears our boundless regret. He sowed in brotherhood and fellowship. The dew of love and sympathy moistens the eyes of his brethren and enriches their hearts with blessed understanding of his virtues and good qualities. His record as Grand Chaplain is that of a life well spent in the service of his fellowmen. All who knew him loved him and honored him for his strength of character, his broad sympathies and for the earnestness with which he labored for the betterment of humanity. He was a loving and faithful husband and patriotic citizen."

As stated above, after the Regiment was disbanded, the warrant was returned in accordance with the injunction. Bro. Newton could have returned the charter at the time he returned to his wife's home in Brooklyn, New York after the war, where he registered as a citizen of the United States.

In 1877 the two Grand Lodges of New York (National and Independent) consolidated and the warrant became the property of the present Prince Hall Grand Lodge of New York.

Not much is known of the subsequent career of this Army Lodge. Its minutes and paraphernalia were presumably lost with records of the Grand Lodge, which disappeared after the consolidation.

This has been a brief look at Prince Hall Freemasonry and the Civil War. The mere fact that Prince Hall Freemasons were indeed holding Lodge within the lines of the Union Army is remarkable. And, as we shall see in the next chapter, Prince Hall Freemasonry has maintained

Military Lodges from 1863, when First Sergeant William H. Gray of the 54th Massachusetts Volunteer Infantry became Master of Hayden Lodge in South Carolina, to the present.

REFERENCES FOR PART IV

1. John Hope Franklin, *The Emancipation Proclamation*, (Garden City, N. Y., Doubleday N. Co. Inc. 1966) p. 11.
2. Ibid, p 98
3. *The War of the Rebellion, Official Records of the Union and Confederate Armies*, 128 Vols., (Washington, 1880-1902) 3 sets, 1, 77, 78, 159, cited by Dudley Taylor Cornish, *The Sable Arm* (New York, London Toronto, Longmans, Green and Co., 1956) p. 96.
4. Benjamin Quarles, *The Negro in the Civil War*. (Boston, Little Brown and Company, 1953) p. 101.
5. William Loren Katz, *Eyewitness: The Negro in American History*. (New York, Toronto, London, Pitman Publishing Corporation, 1967) p. 189.
6. Quarles, *op. cit.*, p. 101.
7. "If the friend of our race, the friend of humanity everywhere, whether in America, Europe or Africa, that man who knew no distinction, save merit and virtue, and from whose inspiring counsel the widow, the orphan, the outcast, and even the slave, in his gloomiest hours found comfort and support, (we allude to John A. Andrews, who was never dressed in that now so much dishonored garb, *a white apron)* yet, whose natural love for, and recognition of, the Brotherhod of Man was prompted by the three tenets of our profession as Masons, Brotherly Love, Relief, and Truth, as shown by these memorable words: "I know not what record of sin awaits me in the other world, but this I do know, that I never was so mean as to despise any man, because he was poor, because he was ignorant, or because he was black." And who as Governor, was the first, in his official capacity to recognize us as a Grand Lodge of Masons as he did in 1864." Lewis Hayden, *Grand Lodge Jurisdictional Claim or, War of Races*. (Boston, Edward S. Coombs, 1868) p. 43.
8. Luis F. Emilio, *A History of the Fifty-Fourth Regiment of Massachusetts Volunteer Infantry 1863-1865*. (Boston, The Boston Book Company, 1868) p. 12.
9. Harry E. Davis, *A History of Freemasonry Among Negroes in America*. (Chicago, Charles T. Powner Co., 1946) p. 272.
10. Harold Van Buren Voorhis, *Negro Masonry in the United States*. (New York City, Henry Emmerson, 1940) p.x., Davis, *op. cit.* p. 195.
11. Charles H. Wesley, *The History of the Prince Hall Grand Lodge of Free and Accepted Masons of the State of Ohio 1849-1960*. (Wilberforce, Ohio, Central State College Press, 1961) p. 44.
12. William Hartwell Parham and Jeremiah Arthur Brown, *An Official History of the Most Worshipful Grand Lodge of Free and Accepted Masons for the State of Ohio*. (1906) p. 267.
13. William Schouler, *A History of Massachusetts in the Civil War*. (Boston, E. P. Dutton & Co., Publishers, 1868) p. 509.

14. *Ibid*, p. 509.

15. Voorhis, *op. cit.*, p. 42; Davis, *op. cit.*, p. 185-186; and John Black Vrooman and Allen E. Roberts, *Sword and Trowel*. (Fulton, Missouri, The Ovid Bell Press, 1964) p. 100.

16. Emilio, *op. cit.*, p. 129.

17. On September 29, 1884, on the occasion of the 100th Anniversary of the granting of Warrant No. 459 to African Lodge, George H. Williams, Black Historian, presented an oration to the Prince Hall Grand Lodge of Massachusetts.

18. Military Service Records, National Archives, Washington, D.C.

19. Lewis Hayden, *Caste Among Masons*. (Boston, Edward S. Coombes & Company, 1866) p. 6-7.

20. Proceedings of the Caucasian Grand Lodge of Massachusetts of September 13, 1876.

21. Harry A. Williamson, *A Chronological History of Prince Hall Masonry* (Published in the New York Age, 1934) p. 90.

22. William H. Grimshaw, *Official History of Freemasonry Among the Colored People in North America*. (New York, Macoy Publishing & Masonic Supply Co., 1903) p. 263.

23. J. N. Conna, *Historical Footprints of Modern Freemasonry Among the Colored Man in the United States and Canada* (Privately published.)

24. Emilio, *op. cit.*, p. 313.

25. *Ibid*, p. 365.

26. *Ibid*, p. 365.

27. *Ibid*, p. 330.

28. Charles H. Wesley, *Richard Allen—Apostle of Freedom*. (Washington, D.C., The Associated Publishers, Inc., 1935) p. 235.

29. Benjamin Quarles, *Black Abolitionists* (London, Oxford, New York, Oxford University Press, 1969) p. 102 & 107.

30. Frank A. Rollins, *Life and Public Services of Martin R. Delany* (New York, Arno Press & New York Times, 1969) p. 153.

31. Daniel A. Payne, *Recollections of Seventy Years*. (New York, Arno Press & New York Times, 1969) p. 160. Payne records "The Major was a man of fine talents and more than ordinary attainments. He traveled much, and traveled with eyes and ears open. Therefore he knew much of men and things in Africa, England, Scotland, and America—in Canada as well as in the United States. He studied medicine at Harvard University, and would have been rich if he had practiced it as a profession for life. But he was too much of a cosmopolitan to stick to it. His oratory was powerful, at times magnetic. If he had studied law, made it his profession, kept an even course, and settled down in South Carolina, he would have reached the Senate-Chamber of that proud state. But he was too intensely African to be popular, and therefore multiplied enemies where he could have multiplied friends by the thousands. Had his love for humanity been as great as his love for his

race, he might have rendered his personal influence co-extensive with that of Samuel R. Ward in his palmiest days, or that of Frederick Douglass at the present time. The Major was a great admirer of ancient heroes, especially those of Hamitic extraction. Therefore he named all of his six children after them. Toussaint L' Ouverture, Alexander Dumas, St. Cyprian (also the name of Delany's Lodge) Soulouque, Faustin, and Ethiopia are the names of his five sons and one daughter.

32. Military Service Records, National Archives, Washington, D.C.

33. Report of Lt. Edward M. Stoeber, Washington, D.C., National Archives, July 24, 1865, Record Group 94 cited by William Loren Katz, *Eye-Witness: The Negro in American History.* p. 252-253.

34. William Schouler, *op. cit.,* p. 585.

35. Lewis Hayden, *Caste Among Masons,* an Address at the Festival of St. John the Evangelist, December 27, 1865 (Boston, Edward S. Coombs & Company, 1866) p. 70-71.

36. *Ibid,* p. 71-72.

37. Emilio, *op. cit.,* p. 252.

38. *Ibid,* p. 283.

39. *Ibid,* p. 312.

40. Harry A. Williamson, *The Prince Hall Primer* (New York, Macoy Publishing & Masonic Supply Co., 1952) p. 21.

NOTE: Mackey, years later wrote that "racial prejudice existed in American Masonry, but it would be unjust to charge the organized Masonic institution because of the personal prejudice of some of its members. And that the Prince Hall Lodge of Boston, whether originally legal or not, certainly lost is legality, subsequently, if it ever had it. And whether legal or not, as a particular Lodge, it could, under no law of Masonry recognized in this country, assume of its own volition the functions of a Grand Lodge. Therefore all subordinate Lodges formed under its obedience are irregular and their members clandestine." (*Voice of Masonry,* Volume 14, 1878, p. 423.) While on the other hand, he refrains from a like declaration of clandestinism when he records that the Kilwinning Lodge (Scotland) seceded from the Grand Lodge and established itself as an independent body. It organized Lodges in Scotland, and several instances are on record of its issuing Charters as Mother Kilwinning Lodge to Lodges in foreign countries. Thus, it granted one to a Lodge in Virginia in 1758. (Page 518, *Encyclopeida of Freemasonry* by Albert Mackey (New York, Macoy Publishing & Masonic Supply Co., 1950). On the subject of German Lodges, he records that "a curious feature of the growth of the Craft in Germany is the number of independent Masonic bodies which, with or without special authority, exercise control over other Lodges. There are also several independent Lodges in existence. The first of these Grand Lodges was probably the Zu Den Drei Weltkugeln (Three Globes), opened in Berlin by the Command of Frederick, who afterwards assumed the position of Grand Master as often as his military duties permitted." (Mackey, *op. cit.*, p. 402.) But yet Mackey would state that "there is a well known maxim of the law which says *Omnis innovatis plus novitate perturbat quam utiliate prodest*, that is, every innovation occasions more harm and disarrangement by its novelty than benefit by its actual utility. This maxim is peculiarly applicable to Freemasonry, whose system is opposed to all innovations." (Mackey, *op. cit.*, p. 486.) This writer wonders how Mackey could attack Prince Hall Freemasonry without attacking the Mother Kilwinning and Three Globes Lodges, and the innovations of the American system of so-called exclusive territorial jurisdiction.

41. Charles Bernard Fox, *Record of the Service of the 55th Regiment of Massachusetts Volunteer Infantry.* (Printed for the Regimental Association by John Wilson & Son, 1868) p. 25, and William Hartwell Parham and Jeremiah Arthur Brown, *op. cit.*, p. 28.

42. Lewis Hayden, *Caste Among Masons*, p. 7. "That at Charleston, S.C., has been duly warranted and constituted under the name of Hayden Lodge, No. 8. Its master is Brother Robert S. Lord. ...I found in Charleston, S.C., a still higher class of people, even, than at Petersburg, as regards general education, the mechanical arts, and the elements which tend to make a first class society. In proof of this, I have brought with me a list of applications for initiaitons to their Lodges, the signers of which will compare favorably with the members of any Masonic Ldoge, either white or black, in the United States, whether we take into consideration proficiency in the mechanical arts, or social and mental endowments. Of the people of Charleston whether in the order or not, I am constrained to say, that the many acts of kindness and the generous hospitality received at their hands, during my sojourn among them, have made an impression upon my heart, which neither time nor changing fortune can ever efface." *The Atlantic Monthly* reported that "...a branch of the Masonic brotherhood, which has a few sickly subordinate Lodges and a state lodge; for this a charter was obtained, I am informed, from the State of Massachusetts. These colored Masons are not recognized by the white lodges or grand body of the State." *South Carolina Society, The Atlantic Monthly*, June 1877, p. 683.

43. John Black Vrooman and Allen E. Roberts, *Sword and Trowel—The Story of Traveling and Military Lodges* (Missouri: Missouri Lodge of Research, 1964). 101.

44. Harry E. Davis, *A History of Freemasonry Among Negroes in America.* (United Supreme Council. A.A.S.R., Northern Jurisdiction, U.S.A. (Prince Hall Affiliation, Inc., 1946) p. 185.

45. *Record of Service of Connecticut Men in the Army and Navy of the United States during the War of the Rebellion* by the Adjutant General. p. 859.

46. In the *Complete History of Widow's Son Lodge No. 11 F & A.M. of Brooklyn, New York* by Ira S. Holder, Sr., and Courtenay L. Weltshire

(page 20) appears a notice or summons dated November 19, 1866, notifying the Lodge that the Annual Grand Communication would be held on December 26, 1866, and signed by the same Samuel J. Scottron as Grand Master. The signatures on the warrant of Phoenix Lodge and the summons of Widow's Son Lodge are the same. In the Transaction of the PHLORONY (Prince Hall Lodge of Research of New York) (Volume 1, 1943) under title, *Men of Mark in Prince Hall Freemasonry*, presented by Harry A. Williamson (page 32). "Samuel R. Scottron...was an officer of the New York State adjunct of the National Grand Lodge, also, he was actively associated with Dr. Peter W. Ray in the Scottish Rite. He was a resident of Brooklyn, N.Y. and a manufacturer of imitation marble."

47. Alexander Herritage Newton, D.D., *Out of the Briars*. (Florida, Mnemosyne Publishing Co., Inc. 1969)

48. *Ibid*, Preface, p. viii.

49. *Ibid*, p. 28. In William H. Grimshaw's, *Official History of Freemasonry among the Colored People in North America*. (New York: Books for Libraries Press, 1971), p. 244, states that "in 1859, Paul Drayton, Grand Master of New York, granted a warrant to nine Master Masons residing in Hartford, Connecticut, to organize a new Lodge of Master Masons, under the title of Widow's Son Lodge, F. & A.M. which was duly established and chartered by the Grand Lodge of New York." This date however does not agree with the *Prince Hall Masonic Yearbook* (Grand Master's Conference of Prince Hall Masons, 1968)' p. 46., which gives a date of 1849. Bro. Newton may have been raised in one of the Lodges set up in the state by New York.

50. *Ibid*, p. 28. Also, Davis, *op. cit.*, p. 244., states that in 1864 the Supreme Council of the United States, (Prince Hall Affiliation) was organized in New York City with Ill. Peter W. Ray as its Grand Commander.

51. *Ibid*, p. 112. James Milton Turner, outstanding Prince Hall Mason from the M.W. Prince Hall Grand Lodge F. & A.M. of Missouri, was a Negro leader and Minister to Liberia. He helped to raise funds and served as trustee to Lincoln University in Jefferson City, Missouri. He secured $75,000 from Congress for the Cherokee Nation for its Negro tribesmen. There is a Lodge in Missouri named after him.

52. *Ibid*, p. 27. William Paul Quinn began his work as a circuit preacher and missionary of the African Methodist Episcopal Church in Western Pennsylvania, Ohio, Indiana and Illinois and by 1844 he had established 47 churches with a membership of two thousand. Peter M. Bergman, *The Chronological History of the Negro in America*. (New York, Harper & Row, 1969) p. 145. Bro. Quinn was a Chaplain for the National Compact Grand Lodge.

53. See Reference 46.

54. Aldrage B. Cooper, *Footprints of Prince Hall Masonry in New Jersey* (New York, Press of Henry Emmerson, 1957) p. 193.

55. Voorhis, *op. cit.*, between p. 44-45.

V

THOSE MAGNIFICENT MASONIC BUFFALO SOLDIERS

The annals of Military Freemasonry may be described as a veritable romance of "good-will upon earth." This is not to deny to the civil(ian) records of the Craft the possessions of an abundant fund of varied interest on the same excellent lines both in their archeological and historical aspects. But, after all, the warrior or member of the Brotherhood are those who have always carried its influence into what are still the most strenuous paths of romance—those of military adventure.

Fighting Freemasons, The Influence of the Brotherhood in War
by J. H. Manners Howe, Dec. 11, 1909

Prince Hall Freemasonry from its inception has played a major role in sustaining Black America. Nowhere is this more evident than in the wars fought by Blacks for America. As has been seen in the previous chapter, the Black soldier brought with him not only his religion and his desire for true freedom, but his Masonry as well.

To better understand the concept of Military Lodges and their tradition, it must be made clear that they had long existed in the British Army. Prince Hall himself was raised in a Military Lodge. The earliest warrant creating a traveling, or movable Lodge, was issued in 1732 by the Grand Lodge of Ireland (1) and by the year 1813, the time of the union of the two Grand Lodges in England, there were approximately 352 Military Lodges among the Grand Lodges of Ireland, Scotland and England. (2)

Though all Military Lodges supported the traditions of the Fraternity in the upholding of Masonic obligations and ritualistic work, their failure to maintain minutes of their communications or submit reports to their Grand Lodges is the reason that there is little known of their existence within the Prince Hall fraternity. Some Military Lodges ceased to work owing to the loss of their warrants. The loss was often due to leaving their property behind when moving from one station to another and also to their sheer inability to continue their labors because of too few members.

Yet, Prince Hall Freemasonry continued its military tradition. After the Civil War the National Grand Lodge, or Compact, issued the following guidelines to govern such Lodges:

REGULATIONS OF MILITARY LODGES

It being essential to the interest of the Craft, that all military Lodges should be strictly confined to the purposes for which their warrants were originally obtained, and as very great abuse may arise from the improper initiations of Masons by such Lodges, every warrant, therefore, which is held by a military Lodge, shall be forfeited, unless the following laws be complied with, in addition to those specified under the rule regulating subordinate Lodges.

1st. No warrant shall be granted for the establishment of a military Lodge, without the consent of the Commanding Officer of the regiment, battalion or company, to which it is to be attached, having first been obtained.

2nd. No military Lodge shall, on any pretense, initiate into Masonry, any inhabitant or sojourner at any town or place at which its members may be stationed, or through which they may be marching, or any person who does not, at the time, belong to the military profession, nor any military person below the rank of corporal, except as serving brethren or by dispensation from the Grand Master. [The words "corporal and serving brethren" were stricken out and replaced with "proper and acceptable material only to be the standard."]

3rd. When any military Lodge under the Constitution of a M.W.G. Lodge, under the jurisdiction of this M.W.N.G. Lodge, shall be in foreign parts, it shall conduct itself so as not to give offence to the Masonic authority of the country or place in which it may sojourn, never losing sight of the duties it owes to the Grand Lodge, to which communication is ever to be made, and all fees and dues regularly transmitted.

4th. If the regiment, battalion, or military company to which a military Lodge is attached be disbanded or reduced, the brethren shall take care that the warrant be carefully transmitted to the Grand Lodge, that it may not fall into improper hands, but if a competent number of the brethren remain together, they may apply for another warrant, of the same number, to be holden as a civil Lodge, at such place as may be convenient, and which may be approved by the Grand Master. Such warrant to be granted without any additional expense.(3)

Historically, Military Lodges have had their ups and downs. Most Lodges faded out, with occasional restorations, after a more or less prolonged life. This brevity, however regrettable, was the inevitable outcome of the military life, the constant traveling from station to station, war, and the death or retirement of members.

After the Civil War, there would ride into the Indian Territory of the West the greatest military Cavalry unit America ever assembled.

These were *"The Buffalo Soldiers,"* so named by the Indians they fought. The troopers' hair reminded them of Buffalo fur. Magnificent Black men, who would ride across the frontiers of the early west and into the pages of the history of an often ungrateful nation.

Much has been written about these Troopers—their hardships and successes. The winners of eighteen Congressional Medals of Honor; but very little is known of the Prince Hall Masonic Lodges that sustained them. Harry A. Williamson, Harry E. Davis, Harold V. B. Voorhis, John Black Vrooman and Allen E. Roberts are the exceptions among historians having briefly mentioned the existence of such Lodges in their books. (4)

The famous 9th and 10th Cavalry Regiments were organized in 1866. (5) The duties of the 9th were to protect the stagecoach lines, to establish law and order along the Mexican border, and to keep the Indians on reservations. The 10th, some would say, became better known than the 9th for their frequent encounters with hostile Indians. This may or may not be true, but what is true, together they became a legend in their own time.

The first Masonic Lodge attached to either unit was with the 10th Cav. Dispensation for a Lodge was granted in 1883 by the Prince Hall Grand Lodge of Texas under the title of Baldwin Lodge at Camp Rice, Texas.(6) The Lodge was probably named after T.A. Baldwin, a Caucasian Captain, Commanding Officer of a Troop. Baldwin was born in New Jersey and became a Brigadier-General and Commanding Officer of the 10th Cav. It was under his command, that the 10th Cav., led by Black non-commissioned officers, saved Col. Teddy Roosevelt, a Mason, and his Rough Riders from being massacred at the famous charge up San Juan Hill.

Camp Rice was initially a railroad construction camp, but was selected as a site for a camp of one company of Cavalry in 1882. It became the home of A Troop, 10th Cav. for a time.(7) The base camp for the regiment was actually Fort Davis, Texas, and it is here where Baldwin Lodge was first situated.

In the spring of 1885, the Regiment with the Lodge now numbered 16 by its Mother Grand Lodge of Texas (8) moved into the military department of Arizona and the land of the Apache, where Geronimo, The Kid, Mangus, Cochise, and other Chieftains held sway.(9)

By 1887 the Lodge was located at Fort Verde, Arizona Territory, with 13 members on its roll, and by 1888 it had 16 members with four Past Masters. One, Bro. Benj. F. Potts was commissioned District Deputy Grand Master, (10) and Arizona became the Sixth Masonic District of the Texas Jurisdiction.(11)

In 1889, the Lodge moved to Fort Apache and found another Prince Hall Lodge from a sister jurisdiction attached to another Troop within this Cavalry unit and also to the 24th Infantry Regiment. This Lodge, Eureka Military No. 135, was one of two Military Lodges chartered by the Prince Hall Grand Lodge of Missouri.(12)

It would be between these two Lodges from two different Prince Hall jurisdictions, sharing the same Fort within the same military units, that the first demit would be recorded. The member having this distinction was Bro. Charles H. Chinn, recorded as Senior Warden of Eureka No. 135 in 1885 (13) and later Secretary of Baldwin No. 16, having demitted to the Texas Lodge, Nov. 5, 1891.

In 1895, Bro. James A. Brown, Treasurer and long time member of Baldwin No. 16 is recorded in the proceedings of that Grand Lodge as having died Feb. 5, 5895(A.L.) (1895)(14)

His death, the first for the Lodge, needs more than just passing mention, as it reveals the hardships that these units faced.

Orders, 2, Troop I, Feb. 11

It becomes the sad duty of the Commanding Officer, Troop I to add to its record the tragic death, by freezing of 1st Sergt. James Brown. His life was sacrificed in the frightful storm of the 5th inst., while attempting to return from an authorized absence of a few hours to the town of Havre. His riderless horse, returning to the post, announced the melancholy news of his death. Sergt. Brown joined the regiment as a recruit in July, 1867, and was assigned to Troop I on its organization, Aug. 1867. He was appointed corporal Jan. 1, 1868, promoted to sergeant Jan. 1, 1869, appointed first sergeant Aug. 1, 1872, in which position he served until his death, when he was, in date of warrant, probably, the senior first sergeant on the active list of the Army. He took part in every campaign and in all of the numerous engagements against hostile Indians in which the Troop has participated since its organization, and was severly wounded by an arrow in battle with overwhelming numbers of Cheyennes on Beaver Creek, Kansas, Oct. 18, 1868. For his conspicuous gallantry on the occasion he was recommended for a medal of honor by Gen. Eugene A. Carr, who was a witness of his bravery. He was in every sense a gallant and efficient soldier. He knew no fear, and there were no difficulties too great for him to attempt to surmount. His untimely death has deprived the regiment and the Army of a model soldier.

S. L. Woodward
Captain 10th Cav., Commanding, Troop I(15)

Concerning the Beaver Creek incident, Troop I was escorting Major General Carr, of the 5th Cavalry, to his command at Beaver Creek. On the march the Troop was attacked by a force of about 500 Indians. After proceeding, regardless of the enemy's firing and yelling, far enough to gain a suitable position, the command was halted, and the wagons were corralled close together, and the Troop was rushed inside at a gallop.

The Troop then dismounted, tied their horses to the wagons and formed outside the corral of wagons. There followed a volley which drove the Indians back as though they were thrown from a cannon. A number of warriors, showing more bravery than the others, undertook to stand their ground. Nearly all of these, together with their ponies, were killed. Three dead warriors lay within fifty yards of the wagons. The Indians were demoralized by these results; they did not renew the attack.(16)

Baldwin Lodge, like so many Military Lodges that preceded it, would cease to exist. The proceedings of the Prince Hall Grand Lodge of Texas traces its movements to Fort Leavenworth, Kansas 1893-94, Fort Assinniboine, Chouteau County and, finally, to Montana, 1895-97. From there, no mention is made of this historical first Military Lodge attached to the Buffalo Soldiers.

The Prince Hall Grand Lodge of Missouri began a Chapter unparalleled in Black Masonic history. It became the "Mother" Grand Lodge of the four Black units then authorized by Congress. These units were the 9th and 10th Cavalry and the 24th and 25th Infantry.

To this Grand Lodge would go the credit of chartering an unbelievable number of Military Lodges and establishing its Masonic jurisdictions in Cuba and the Philippines. Not much is known of these Lodges, their records having long since vanished. But the fact that they did exist is of historical importance.

The first Military Lodge chartered by Missouri was Eureka No. 135. It was established before 1888; the actual date is not known. It was attached to the 10th Cavalry; its members came also from the 24th Infantry.

The second Military Lodge chartered by Missouri was Adventure No. 136. It was attached to Troops H and L of the 9th Cavalry at Fort Wingate, New Mexico. Of interest concerning this Lodge, recorded in the proceedings of Missouri for the year 1900 is: "that as the papers referring to the death of Bro. Washington Henry cannot be completed by the Lodge which has been ordered to China..." Whether this Lodge actually went to China is not known, as there is no further mention of it within the proceedings of this Grand Lodge, but it is doubtful.

The next Military Lodge organized was Gillispie No. 140, which at one time was attached to the 25th Infantry at Fort Missoula, Montana. It was later recognized and attached to Troop K, 9th Cavalry at Fort Du Chesne, Utah.

Military Lodge No. 152 followed. It was at one time also located at Fort Du Chesne and was tranferred to Fort Grant, Arizona and later moving to Fort Robinson, Nebraska. There is a possibility that it was likewise attached to the 9th Cavalry; however, information on the exact military unit is unavailable.

The fifth Lodge, Military No. 153, was organized at Fort Grant. Its membership was composed of Troopers from Hqs, A, B, and M Troop, of the 9th Cavalry.

The one Lodge of which photographs have been found with the members in full Masonic regalia was Joppa No. 150 attached also to the 9th Cavalry. It was at one time at Fort Walla Walla, Washington, Fort Riley, Kansas, and the Philippines. The photographs are historic as they are the only known photographs of their kind in existence.

Continuing its uninterrupted sequence of organizing Military Lodges, Missouri charterd Minnachuduza Military Lodge U.D. at Niobrora, Nebraska on May 27, 1906. It was organized with its officers and eleven others. The dedication of the Lodge was performed by the Master, Wardens and members of Military Lodge No. 135.

While outside the Continential United States, the District Deputy Grand Master, Bro. W. H. Loving, organized Manila Military Lodge No. 63, March 5, 1906, it being recorded as the second Military Lodge in Manila. John M. McCarthy Lodge No. 50 chartered six years later at Schofield Barracks in Honolulu, Hawaii and attached to the 25th Infantry, together with the Lodges in the Phillipine Islands would make up the 20th Masonic District of the Prince Hall Grand Lodge of Missouri.(17) The Grand Lodge often re-used the numbers which had been assigned to defunct Lodges sometimes creating problems of identification. Such is the case of Eureka Military Lodge No. 135 at Fort Robinson, Nebraska, chartered between 1901 and 1903; while in 1912 another Lodge, Oriental, would also be numbered 135 and stationed in Manila.(18) Yet it would seem that the Grand Lodge itself did not have any problems in the often duplication of numbers.

In 1916, Eureka Lodge No. 135, at the time assigned to Fort Huachuca, Arizona, was reorganized, renamed and renumbered ending the confusion over two Lodges carrying the same number. Eureka thus became Malta Lodge No. 138 and the Grand Master, Nelson C. Crews, would express relief in his address to the Grand Lodge, that none of the members of the Lodge "were lost during the bloody conflict of the 10th cavalry to which they belonged at the Battle of Carrizel."(19) It was at this battle that a controversial order by General "Black Jack" Pershing, a Freemason, (2), resulted in the death, capture and humiliation of many soldiers from the Tenth Cavalry.(21) Members of the Lodge participated in the battle, which records the last major cavalry charge by American Troopers on the Continent.

The last Military Lodge recorded by Missouri, was charted in 1919 at Columbus, New Mexico, being Tyre Military Lodge No. 143, attached to the 25th Infantry.(22)

The Prince Hall Grand Lodge of Missouri was proud of its Military Lodges stationed across western United States, Hawaii and the Philippines. Throughout its proceedings are echoed the pride felt by the Grand Lodge for its military Master Masons:

> "We feel proud of our boys who made splendid records for their race. The Negro can be depended upon at all times when called upon to defend the Stars and Stripes. History shows the Negro has always made good as a soldier, and will always make good when given the opportunity."(23)

In keeping with that pride, during the Christmas of 1917, the Grand Lodge of Missouri mailed Christmas presents to its 350 military Masons throughout the United States and overseas. The gifts consisted of bath towels, wash cloths, face towels, smoking tobacco, dressing cases, writing papers and envelopes. The proceedings of the Grand Lodge, published in full, many of the letters of thanks from the soldiers, Freemasons all, who received the gifts. Such events exemplified the feelings of the Craft in Missouri.

Late in the 1930's Missouri proudly carried four military Lodges on its register: John M. McCarthy Lodge No. 52; Malta Military Lodge No. 138; Tyre Military Lodge No. 143; and Joppa Military Lodge No. 150.

So, following the tradition of their brethren in the Civil War, the Prince Hall Freemasons carried their Lodges with their military units as they carried their religion and racial strength. It is historically the essential institution and characteristic which sustained the race for over 200 years.

Blacks, at the turn of the century, had very little to help sustain their faith in themselves, except the pride that they took in the Ninth and Tenth Cavalry and the Twenty-Fourth and Twenty-Fifth Infantry. The Army and military life had long occupied a position of relatively greater concern and importance to the Black community and "soldiering" had been an honored career for the few Blacks who were able to enter upon it.

Retired Infantry and Cavalry Sergeants from the above units, as well as the Prince Hall Masonic Lodges in the locality, were often the leading spirits in the Black community life, as can be seen in the case of Lincoln University in Jefferson City, Missouri. It was established with funds given by the enlisted men of regiments of the United States Colored Troops after the Civil War. The Prince Hall Grand Lodge of Missouri continues a special relationship with this Black school.

Recorded in the 1976 *Prince Hall Yearbook* (List of Masonic Lodges) published off and on by the Conference of Prince Hall Grand Masters, are listed more than 60 Military Lodges. The Military Lodges are located in Asia, England, Germany, Belgium, The Netherlands, Italy, Taiwan, Thailand, Japan, Korea, Guam, The Philippines and wherever the United States maintains a military presence. These Lodges, chartered by ten Prince Hall Grand Lodges, are often classed as "the finest within the Prince Hall family!"

Missouri, the "Mother" of Military Lodges, continued its tradition by maintaining Lodges in the Canal Zone; at Athens, Greece; Fort Leonard Wood; and Whiteman Air Force Base in Missouri.

Joppa Military Lodge No. 150—P.I., Harrison Henderson, W. M.

The M. W. Grand Lodge of Missouri ✦ Its Jurisdiction, Greeting:

WISDOM. STRENGTH. FRATERNITY.

Know Ye, That by virtue of the power and authority in us vested, we do hereby constitute and appoint our worthy and well-beloved brethren _____, *Worshipful Master,* _____, *Senior Warden,* and _____, *Junior Warden,* of a Lodge, to be called _____ No. _____ to be holden in _____ And we do further authorize and empower our said trusty and well-beloved brethren, _____ to ADMIT, ENTER, PASS AND RAISE FREEMASONS, according to the most ancient and honorable custom of the Royal Craft in all ages and nations throughout the known world, and not contrarywise: and we do further empower and appoint the said _____ and their successors, to hear and determine all and singular matters and things relating to the Craft within the jurisdiction of the said Lodge, with the assistance of the members of said Lodge. And lastly we do hereby authorize and empower our said trusty and well-beloved brethren, _____ to install their successors, (being first duly elected and chosen) to whom they shall deliver this Warrant, and to invest them with all the powers and dignities to their offices respectively belonging, and such successors, &c., &c. Such installation to be upon or near St. John the Baptist's day, during the continuance of this Lodge, forever. PROVIDED ALWAYS, That the said above named brethren, and their successors, pay due respect to this Most Worshipful Grand Lodge, and the ordinances thereof; otherwise this Warrant to be of no force or effect.

GIVEN in open Grand Lodge, under the hands of our Most Worshipful Grand Officers, and the Seal of our Grand Lodge, at _____ this _____ day of _____

A. L. 59___ A. D. 19___

Attest:

_____ Grand Sec'y.

_____ D. G. M.
_____ S. G. W.
_____ G. W.
_____ G. T.

Charter of Malta Military Lodge No. 138.

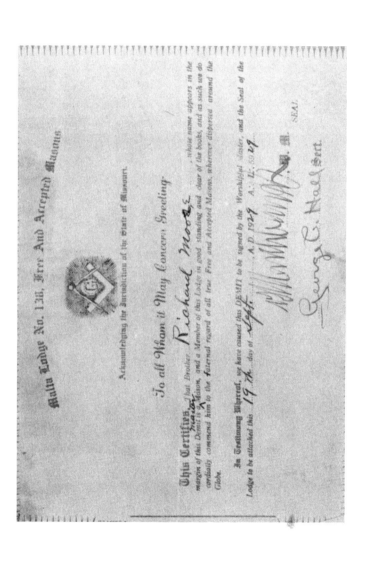

Demit issued by Malta Military Lodge No. 138.

Ft. Leavenworth, Kansas
October 23, 1929.

To the Worshipful Master, Wardens and Brethren of
Eureka Lodge No. 27, A.F. & A.M., Brethren: I hereby apply for
fraternal Affiliation with your Lodge.

I am a Master Mason in good standing, hailing from
Malta Military Lodge No. 138 A.F. & A.M., of the Masonic
Jurisdiction of Missouri, and with this petition submit my
dimit from said Lodge.
I am, fraternally,

Richard Moore

Fort Leavenworth, Kansas.

Letter from a member of Malta Military Lodge No. 138 submitting his demit.

Officers Joppa Military Lodge No. 150. Frank D. Clinton, Master, Ft. D. A. Russell, Wyoming. ("World Renowned Ninth U.S. Cavalry.")

REFERENCES FOR PART V

1. Albert G. Mackey, *Encyclopedia of Freemasonry.* (New York, Macoy Publishing & Masonic Supply Co., Inc., 1966) p. 667.

2. Frederic Adams, MA., D. Litt, *Traveling* (or Ambulatory) *Military Lodges*, (Transactions, The American Lodge of Research F. & A.M., Vol. VII, No. 2, p. 199, January 29, 1958 to December 29, 1958.)

3. Proceedings of the Sixth Triennial Session of the Most Worshipful National Grand Lodge of Free and Accepted Ancient York Masons of the U.S.A., held in the City of Baltimore, October A.D., 1865, p. 25.

4. *A Chronological History of Prince Hall Masonry 1784-1932* by Harry A. Williamson, p. 85; Harold Van Buren Voorhis, *Negro Masonry in the United States* (New York, Henry Emmerson Press, 1949) p. 42; Harry E. Davis, *A History of Freemasonry Among Negroes in America.* (United Supreme Council, A.A.S.R., Northern Jurisdiction, U.S.A., Prince Hall Affiliation, Inc., 1946) p. 185.

5. 28th day of July 1866, U.S. Congress and General Orders No. 92, A.G.O., Nov. 23, 1866.

6. Proceedings of the Prince Hall Grand Lodge of Texas 1883, page 51, henceforth called Proceedings of Texas.

7. John M. Carroll, *The Black Military Experience in the American West* (New York, Liveright Publishing Co., 1971), p. 113-4.

8. Proceedings of Texas 1885, p. 47.

9. Carroll, *op. cit.*, p. 137.

10. Proceedings of Texas, 1888, p. 30.

11. *Ibid.*

12. Proceedings of Prince Hall Grand Lodge of Missouri, 1888, p. 109. Henceforth called Proceedings of Missouri.

13. Proceedings of Missouri, 1885, p. 109.

14. Proceedings of Texas, 1895, p. 105.

15. Army & Navy Register, The U.S. Military Gazette, Washington, D.C., Vol. XVII, No. 8, Feb. 23, 1895, p. 120.

16. Carroll, *op. cit.*, p. 83.

17. Proceedings of Missouri, 1917, p. 132.

18. Proceedings of Missouri, 1913, p. 145.

19. Proceedings of Missouri, 1916, p. 22.

20. John J. Pershing was a member of Lincoln Lodge No. 19, Lincoln, Nebraska, receiving degrees on Dec. 4, 11, and 22, 1888. He received his 50 year award on Jan. 5, 1939. On Sept. 30, 1941 he was made an honorary member of the Grand Lodge of Missouri (Caucasian) and the certificate was presented to him by Harry S. Truman, then Senator, at Walter Reed Hospital, Feb. 24, 1942. In 1919 he was made an honorary member of Stanbury Lodge No. 24, Washington, D.C. Exalted in Lincoln Chapter No. 6, R.A.M. March 28, 1894 and knighted in Mount Moriah Commandery No. 4,

K.T., Dec. 3, 1894, both of Lincoln, Nebr. In 1943 he laid a wreath on the Tomb of the Unknown Soldier at the Knight Templar rites. Received the 32⁰ A.A.S.R. (SJ) at Wheeling, W. Va., April 9, 1920 and 33⁰, in Washington, D.C. on Jan. 6, 1930. Member of Sesostris Shrine Temple, Lincoln and New York Court No. 30, Royal Order of Jesters. Died July 15, 1948. William R. Denslow, *10,000 Famous Freemasons*, reprinted in the Transactions of the Missouri Lodge of Research (Trenton, Mo. 1958) p. 331.

21. John M. Carroll, *The Black Military Experience in the American West* (New York, Liveright, 1971) pp. 493-494.

22. Proceedings of Missouri, 1919, p. 132.

23. Proceedings of Missouri, 1919, p. 24.

VI

NIGGERDOM IN REGALIA

[From Pomeroy's Democrat, August 26, 1871]

"In the proceedings of Missouri in 1872, there is much interesting matter concerning a controversy with a man by the name of F. G. Tisdall, the Masonic editor of a New York City newspaper known as *Pomeroy's Democrat*. A news dispatch from Natchez, Miss., tells about the formation of a nigger Lodge called H. R. Revels Lodge, etc. That dispatch was dated March 9, 1871, but on the date of August 26, following, there was published an editorial bearing the caption of 'Niggerdom in Regalia.' Brother Clark replied to the same in very strong language both through letter and in the proceedings for 1872, under the heading of 'An attack on me and the Legitimacy of Masonry Among Colored Men.' One must read all the matter in order to appreciate the attitude of Clark's opponent."

Harry A. Williamson (1)

"January 15th, 1872. H. R. Revels Lodge No. 36, Natchez, Mississippi. I am happy to say I found the brethren all hard at work, under influence of that truly Masonic virtue, circumspection, which makes our beloved order the admonition of all those who have fed upon the moral crumbs that fall from her pure altar."

Alexander Clark (2)

"The man who steals my purse, steals trash;
'Twas mine, tis his, and may be slave to thousands.
But he who pilfers from me my good name
Robs me of that which not enriches him,
But makes me poor indeed."

Shakespeare

"Without this feeling of brotherly love, without this great bond, we can never prosper, more especially in our Order, whose very foundation stone it is. From this feeling, as our footstone, springs all the best and warmest affections; from its practice, every virtue, genuine and not as the world at large construes it; and from it springs truth as a Capstone, the noblest attribute with which an All-wise Providence has endowed us."

F. G. Tisdall (3)

In his book, *The Story of Freemasonry*, W. G. Sibley concedes that race prejudice exists to some extent among Freemasons, although properly it can have no place in so cosmopolitan an institution, and while it has not barred any race from Freemasonry (sic); it has denied recognition in some localities to the Masonic bodies of the Negro race.... (4) The Masonic doctrine of Brotherly love teaches that the whole human species is one family. The high and low, rich and poor, as created by one Almighty Parent and as inhabitants of the same planet, are to aid, support and protect each other. Freemasons are taught that on this principle, Masonry unites men of every country, sect and opinion and conciliates true friendship among those who might otherwise have remained at a perpetual distance. But events recorded in American Masonic history often belittle these honorable and exalted expressions.

"Mississippi," noted the famed and scholarly Prince Hall Freemason, W. E. B. Du Bois, "was a curious state in which to study Reconstruction." Bro. Du Bois recorded that in 1860 there were 353,849 Caucasians and 437,404 Blacks, of whom fewer than 1,000 were free. After the Civil War, the Federal Government required that the State assimilate a voting population of nearly 450,000 former slaves which, in turn, would have a political significance as never seen before. By 1867 there were 46,636 White voters registered compared to 60,137 Black voters. By 1869 the political importance of the Black vote was being felt as Blacks were being elected to positions of importance. (5) And though the spectacle of Blacks voting for public office shocked the White South, Blacks were not represented in proportion to their numbers; yet, their presence in government fostered resentment and complaints of "Negro rule!"

Though the *"Old Charges of Freemasonry"* specifically declare that politics must not be brought within the doors of the Lodge, the Grand Master of the Caucasian Grand Lodge of Mississippi, Thos. S. Gathright, protested Black suffrage within his State and recorded his feelings in his address before the Grand Lodge in 1870.

"Negroes are not Masons, but by the laws of Congress, they are voters. An exciting canvass has just passed in our State, and officers have been elected by the votes of a people, formerly our slaves, and now regarded by us as unfitted for the high dignity and the weighty responsibility of acting the part of legislators....

"The Negroes while they are called, in numbers, the political power of the State, are not responsible for their being in this country, or for occupying the responsible places to which the recent political and social revolution, in our midst, has assigned them. They are ignorant, and out of the seventy thousand who voted in the last election, not one hundred thought or reasoned for themselves, or could think or reason upon the consequences, immediate or remote, that might follow the result." (6)

As a last defiant and pathetic act to a situation they could not understand, control or immediately change, the Grand Lodge voted that the "testimony of a Negro—formerly a slave could not be received in a Lodge trial."(7) How ironic, since the only object of a Masonic trial is to seek the truth. And it is only in a Masonic trial that no advantage is ever permitted to be taken of legal and verbal technicalities, as in a profane court, which often enables the guilty to escape. Yet, if the truth be known by a Black, his testimony would not be permitted by this Grand Lodge.

As the Caucasian Grand Lodge of Mississippi was overreacting to events, two Black Prince Hall Freemasons were elected to high offices by the voters. Bro. (Rev.) Hiram Rhoades Revels became the first Black elected to the United States Senate, filling the unexpired term of Jefferson Davis, former President of the Confederacy and also a non-Mason, (8) and Bro. James R. Lynch became the Secretary of State of Mississippi.

Bro. Revels was born in Fayetteville, North Carolina, of free parents and is recorded as a Past Grand Chaplain of the Prince Hall Grand Lodge of Ohio in 1856 and a member of the Lone Star Lodge No. 2, St. Louis, under the jurisdiction of the Prince Hall Grand Lodge of Missouri. He attended Quaker seminaries in Indiana and Ohio, and Knox College in Illinois. Ordained a minister of the African Methodist Episcopal Church in 1845, he taught and preached in Leavenworth, Kansas and St. Louis, Missouri. It was in St. Louis on January 28, 1858, that he made his famous speech *"An Address Delivered to the Members of the Prince Hall Lodge No. 10 F. & A.M."* (The Lodge then on the register of Ohio, is now numbered No. 1 under Missouri.) (9) During the Civil War he helped organize Black regiments, and was made Chaplain for Black troops in Mississippi. In 1866 he settled in Natchez, Mississippi and was elected Alderman in 1868. He became a State Senator in 1870, and in the same year he was elected to the United States Senate. (10)

Bro. James R. Lynch, Worshipful Master of Lynch Lodge No. 28 F. & A.M., Jackson, Mississippi, was born in Baltimore on January 8, 1839, and in his youth obtained a good education. In 1858 he joined the Presbyterian Church in New York, but soon thereafter was accepted by the African Methodist Episcopal Conference in Indiana. He transferred to Baltimore and in 1863 went to South Carolina as a missionary from the A.M.E. Church to the freedman. From 1866 to June 15, 1867, he was editor of *The Christian Recorder* in Philadelphia. Later he was with the Freedman's Bureau in Mississippi and in 1871 he was elected Secretary of State. (A major speech of Bro. Lynch is recorded in *The Christian Recorder* for May 13, 1865.)

While these events were taking place in Mississippi, the Prince Hall Grand Lodge of Missouri, which was formed after the Civil War (December 20, 1866), began to follow in the footsteps of its Mother Grand Lodge, Ohio, and began to expand its influence and Masonic jurisdiction outside of its State. Missouri chartered Lodges in Leavenworth, and Lawrence, Kansas; (11) Jackson, Vicksburg, Natchez and Greenville, Mississippi. (12)

The Lodge in Vicksburg was Stringer Lodge No. 22, and its Worshipful Master was Thomas W. Stringer. Bro. Stringer was the first Grand Master of the Prince Hall Grand Lodge of Ohio, serving from May 3, 1849 to June 1851. He was born in the year 1811. He was one of the early members of the True American Lodge.

After that Lodge received its warrant from the Prince Hall Grand Lodge of Pennsylvania, Bro. Stringer was appointed District Deputy Grand Master of the territory west of Pittsburgh and, as such, granted a dispensation to certain brethren in New Orleans to open a Lodge. The Lodge, Stringer Lodge No. 3, is under the register of the Prince Hall Grand Lodge of Louisiana.

Bro. Stringer became also the first Grand Master of Prince Hall Masons in the State of Mississippi, serving in that position from 1875 until his death, August 23, 1893. This Grand Lodge is named the Most Worshipful Stringer Grand Lodge F. & A.M. Prince Hall Affiliated in his honor. Missouri also chartered lodges in Memphis, Chattanooga, Knoxville and Brownville, Tennessee; (13) Selma, Alabama; (14) Little Rock and Helena, Arkansas; (15) Keokuk, Muscatine and Des Moines, Iowa; (16) and St. Paul, Minnesota. (17)

Missouri was also extending its Masonic intercourse and correspondence to foreign Grand Lodges such as the Grand Lodges of England, Ireland, Scotland, Canada, Prussia, The Three Globes at Berlin and the Grand Orient of France and Italy. (18) In 1870 alone, more than two hundred letters were sent from Missouri to other Masonic bodies, Prince Hall and Caucasian, around the world. (19)

The Prince Hall Grand Master of Missouri was the dynamic and aggresive Alexander Clark called by many "the eminent orator of Iowa." Bro. Clark was born in Washington County, Pennsylvania, February 25, 1826. His father, who was born a slave, was the son of his master, an Irishman who eventually freed him; his mother was Afro-American. At the age of thirteen he moved to Cincinnati, Ohio, where he learned the barbering business from his uncle, who also sent him to school, where he made considerable proficiency in grammar, arithmetic, geography and natural philosophy. In 1841 he left Cincinnati and went south on the steamer *George Washington* as bartender. In May 1842 he settled in Muscatine, Iowa, which remained his home, and is now listed on the National Register of Historic Places by the United States Government. In Muscatine he conducted a barbershop until 1868. Having accumulated some capital, he invested in real estate, and bought some timber land in the neighborhood of Muscatine, obtaining contracts for the furnishing of wood to steamboats. He also made some speculative investments which proved quite successful. In 1851 he became a member of Prince Hall Lodge No. 10, St. Louis, Missouri. In 1868 he was arched and knighted and elected Deputy Grand Master of the Prince Hall Grand Lodge of Missouri, with H. McGee Alexander being Grand Master. The latter died on April 20, 1868 and Bro. Clark became Grand Master and finished the unexpired term. At the next annual meeting of the Grand Lodge he was elected Grand Treasurer and appointed a delegate to the National Grand Lodge (Compact). In June 1869, he was elected Grand Master and held this office for three consecutive years.

And so the stage is set. On February 27, 1871, Grand Master Clark issued a dispensation to 17 Prince Hall Master Masons in Mississippi for the formation of the H. R. Revels Lodge U.D., at Natchez. On March 29, 1871, under the heading of *"Negroes Trying to REVEL as Masons in Mississippi,"* the following letter appeared in the Masonic column of the *Pomeroy's Democrat* published in New York.

Natchez, March 9, 1871

F. G. Tisdall, 33°, Masonic Editor
Pomeroy's Democrat:

Dear Sir and Bro. Some little time ago an American citizen of African descent—Clark by name—came to this city and established a nigger Lodge, under a dispensation of his own, as Gd. Master of Nig. Masons in Mo. The Lodge is called the H. R. Revels Lodge U.D., in honor of Senator Revels of this State, who claims to be a Kt. T., I am informed. This man claims that the G.

Lodges of Missouri, Iowa, Minnesota and several other States, have recognized the colored Masons—so called—in their jurisdictions, and as I am desired to believe, have extended to them the right hand of fellowship. This being the first intimation I have received of action on the part of those bodies, and from the very questionable source from which the information comes, I am slightly inclined to believe that the man Clark has lied. I am very much afraid that the members of H. R. Revels Lodge U.D., will be too old to enjoy it when they are recognized as Masons by the G. Lodge of Mississippi, or any of its subordinates. Please give us any information as to the action of any G. Lodge on this subject of which you are in possession, in your department of Pomeroy's Democrat, obliging thereby the legitimate Masons of this city.

E. G. De L (20)

Unknown to Grand Master Clark at the time, as the Masonic editor of *Pomeroy's Democrat* attempted to conceal the identity of the writer, there was in fact a Worshipful Master of Harmony Lodge No. 1, located in Natchez on the register of the Caucasian Grand Lodge of Mississippi by the name of E. Geo. De Lap. (21)

F. G. Tisdall, the Masonic Editor, published his answer to De Lap's letter of inquiry.

ANSWER

"The man Clark is a bastard, spurious and illegitimate Mason, and has, as our correspondent was inclinded to believe, lied. There does not exist, a Lodge composed of "American citizens of African descent," in either the United or the 'untied' States, and the Founder of this negro—so called Masonic colony, if he received any fees, Revel-ed at the expense of his fellow descendents of Ham. Neither the Grand Lodges named, nor any other Grand Lodge, has by act or deed recognized the clandestine association of negroes claiming to be Masonic organizations. The negro Clark knows that his statements are false, but no more false than his pretentions to be a Mason. He is a fraud, and a very black one at that. When will the negroes learn to tell the truth?"

Mississippi in 1870 saw a rise in terrorism and anarchy, such as the so-called Knights of the Invisible Empire of the Ku Klux Klan, founded and organized by a former Lieutenant General of the Confederate Army who would be honored by being initiated in a "regular" Masonic Lodge. (22)

The Grand Master of the Caucasian Grand Lodge of Mississippi recorded in the proceedings of that Masonic body, "can we be surprised that members get drunk and shed blood?" (23)

And what manner of man was Fitz Gerald Tisdall, 33⁰ called by the members of his Lodge, a prominent Mason and a brilliant Masonic writer. Tisdall was descended from an old aristocratic Irish family.

His maternal grandfather was Major-General Clark, of the British Army, and he was a cousin of George Canning, at one time Prime Minister of England. His father held a position in the British Civil Service. Tisdall was born in Cork and received a liberal education in Trinity College, Dublin, where he received the degree of A, B. He came to New York City in 1832 and was connected with a sugar house. While thus engaged he went to Brazil, and on his return retired from the house and embarked in the coal trade in 1835. In the meantime he became a zealous member of the Masonic fraternity, and when he retired from business he devoted himself to literary work, writing almost exclusively upon subjects connected with Masonry. He passed through all the degrees of that order, and at the time of his death held the patent of the Supreme Council of the thirty-third degree. (24)

At one time he was the master of one of the oldest Lodges in the United States, St. John's Lodge No. 1 of New York City. It was on this Lodge's Bible (Volume of Sacred Laws), on the 4th day of March 1789, that George Washington, a Freemason and slave owner, the first President of the United States of America, took the oath to support the Constitution of the United States. (25)

As Master of St. John's Lodge No. 1, in 1850, Tisdall in his address before his Lodge stated:

"Brethren, our path through this world is one of dangers, trials, and difficulties, evidently designed by our Grand Master on High, to teach us to look up to him, at all-times, and in all seasons, for his aid, comfort, and support. While he requires our allegiance, and subservience to Him, as the great chief good, he has not only inspired us with, but expects, nay demands from us, the practice of true brotherly love. This virtue, is to act upon the square with our neighbor or fellow man, to render him every kind office, to relieve his wants, and his distresses, to comfort him in his trials, and afflictions, to speak well of him to the world, for nothing can be viler, nothing more base, than to traduce a man behind his back. It is like the villainy of the assassin, who stabs while his victim is unarmed, and unsuspicious of an enemy; for without this feeling of brotherly love, without this great bond, we can never prosper, more especially in our order whose very foundation stone is brotherly love!" (26)

Grand Master Clark wrote that "humility, patience and selfdenial are the three essential qualities of a Master Mason" and sent a reply to the unwarranted attack on him and the Prince Hall Grand Lodge of Missouri.

Muscatine, Iowa

F. G. Tisdall, 33°, Masonic Editor Pomeroy's
Democrat:

Sir:

Will you permit me a reply, through your Masonic columns, to an article in your paper of the 29th of March 1871, under the head of "negroes trying to REVEL as Masons in Mississippi," which article does me great injustice. Passing over your unkind, unchristian, and unmasonic remarks on my personal and Masonic character, and ugly names given me on account of my color, I only trouble you with a word in reply to your correspondent, E. G. De L.

First: Charges that I established a "nigger Lodge" under my "dispensation." This is true enough, excepting bad orthography.

Secondly: That I said that the Grand Lodges of Iowa, Minnesota, Missouri, and other States, had recognized colored Masons in their jurisidictions. This is not true. But I will state for the satisfaction of your correspondent and the Masonic World what I did and said.

First, I organized a Lodge of F. & A.A.Y. Masons in the City of Natchez, Miss., under my dispensation as M. W. G. Master of Masons for the M. W. G. Lodge of Missouri (colored) and her jurisdiction. The name of this Lodge is H. R. Revels, U.D., named in honor of Senator Revels, who is a Sir Knight.

Secondly, I said that I was proud of the Grand Lodges of Illinois and Iowa, in rescinding their black laws prohibiting the initiation, passing and raising of Negroes and Indians to the rights of Masonry. I further stated that the Committee of Foreign Correspondence, for the Grand Lodge of Iowa, had endorsed the exposition of Foreign Correspondence for the Grand Lodge of Minnesota, in regard to the subject of colored Masonry in the United States, which is a virtual recognition to us, and all colored lodges working regularly under the National Compact which emanated from the old African Grand Lodge, chartered in 1784 and 1878, by warrant No. 459, of the Grand Lodge of England. This is what I said, and for the truth of this, I refer your correspondent to the proceedings of the above mentioned Grand Lodges of 1867 and 1870.

I make this statement in vindication of my personal and Masonic character, as colored Masonry, like white Masonry, needs no defense.

A. Clark

Tisdall, in his usual fashion, addressed his Lodge, using these words:

"That the figures of the Sun and Moon, as used by us, are emblematical of the great light of truth discovered to the first man, and thereby implying that as Masons we stand redeemed from darkness—are become the sons of light, acknowledged in profession our adoration of Him who gave light to his works, and as the children of light, we have turned our backs upon darkness, all kinds of obscenity and falsehood." (27)

The moral code of Masonry is still more extensive than that

developed by philosophy. To the requisitions of the law of nature and the law of God, it adds the imperative obligation of a contract. Upon entering the Order, the initiate binds to himself every Mason in the world. Once enrolled among the children of light, every Mason on earth becomes his brother and owes him the duties, the kindness, and the sympathies of a brother.

On everyone he may call for assistance in need, protection against danger, sympathy in sorrow, attention in sickness, and decent burial after death. There is not a Mason in the world who is not bound to go to his relief when he is in danger, if there be a greater probability of saving his life than of losing his own. No Mason can wrong him to the value of anything, knowingly, himself, nor suffer it to be done others, if it be in his power to prevent it. No Mason can speak evil of him, to his face or behind his back. Every Mason must keep his lawful secrets, and aid him in his business, defend his character when unjustly assailed and protect, counsel, and assist his widows and his orphans. What so many thousands owe to him, he owes to each of them. He has solemnly bound himself to be ever ready to discharge this sacred debt. If he fails to do it he is dishonest and forsworn. (28)

On the 26th of August 1871 in the *Pomeroy's Democrat*, F. G. Tisdall, 33⁰ published his infamous "Niggerdom in Regalia."

(From *Pomeroy's Democrat*, August 26th, 1871):

Since our publication of date March 29th ult. of the formation of a so-called Masonic Lodge of Negroes, in Mississippi, named after the colored Senator, "H. R. Revels," by virtue of a Dispensation from an American Citizen of African descent, of the name of Alexander Clark who styled himself Grand Master of the Most Worshipful Grand Lodge of the State of Missouri, though living at Muscatine, Iowa, we have had several communications relative to that, and other assertions of Negroes claiming to be Masonic, asking for information as to their status, history, etc. We also received a long letter from Alexander Clark, headed thusly: The Most Worshipful Grand Lodge for the State of Missouri and its Jurisdiction, Post Office Box 365, Muscatine, Iowa, with a request that we would publish it. As *Pomeroy's Democrat* is a white man's paper, and so far as its Masonic department is concerned, an organ of legitimate Masonry, we declined to publish the communication referred to, as coming from a clandestine source, and returned same to the writer.

The information sought from us from other sources entitled to a hearing in our columns, we shall endeavor to give as concise as possible, especially as but little is known among the regular Fraternity in the United States of the condition of niggerdom in regalia.

So far as we have been able to glean from published proceedings of bodies of negroes claiming to be Masonic, they have, so far as Symbolic Masonry is concerned, Lodges, Grand Lodges, and a National Grand Lodge, the officers of which are designated with all the high sounding titles, in which that imitative race seem to take so great a pride.

These 'colored brudders' have, on more occasions than one, in years gone by, published their list of dignitaries in the press, and probably with the desire of receiving the benefit of our quarter of a million circulation, this year honored us with their notice; but though highly sensible of the intended honor, we most respectfully declined to be the medium of communication between them and the regularly constituted Fraternities of the United States.

While we have every desire to promote the interests of genuine Freemasonry, we have no inclination to give prominence to that which is illegitimate and spurious, and, without designating any affront to the 'sons of Aric,' we cannot consent, directly or indirectly, to elevate them to an equality with the white or dominant race in our columns.

The existence of these so-called Masonic Lodges among the blacks, has never been recognized by any Grand Lodges of Freemasons in the United States. Their origin was not in accordance with the laws of the institution, and it is doubtful to our mind whether their continuance is not, from the material of which they are composed a direct infraction of the Ancient Law which requires of all candidates for initiation into the mysteries of the Society to be 'free born' or 'no bondmen.' "

The authority under which these negro Lodges claim to derive their power is of itself a sufficient evidence of their irregularity; and in order that our readers may be thoroughly posted on the subject, we will give a verbatim copy of the document upon the strength of which they have based their organization.

[Author's note: Here is presented the charter of September 29, 1784 to African Lodge by the Grand Lodge of England.]

Under such an authority as the above is it that the colored population have ventured to establish a National Grand Lodge, which in turn, grants Warrants to State Grand Lodges, and these later to Subordinate Lodges.

The basis upon which the negroes have raised their superstructure according to the laws which prevail among Masons, especially in the United States, is fatally defective, and their work consequently illegitimate. In the first place, the Grand Lodge of England had no right in 1784 to establish a Lodge in Boston, as there was a Grand Lodge, in the second place the Warrant granted in 1784 to the negroes gave them no authority to establish a Grand Lodge of a National Grand Lodge, it being nothing more than an ordinary Lodge Warrant. Thirdly, the Warrant from want of compliance with its provisions, even if it had been legally granted, became forfeited from its failure to make annual returns, and has long since been expunged from the roll of English Lodges. Their recognition, therefore, would be an outrage on Masonic law and usage, and if they are invited here by persons claiming to be regular Masons, it is at the expense of their most solemn covenants.(29)

And so ended the famous "Niggerdom in Regalia." The true philosophy, known and practiced by Solomon, is the basis on which

Masonry is founded.(30) "I am Black but comely, O ye daughters of Jerusalem, as the Tents of Kedar, as the curtains of Solomon. Look not upon me because I am black, because the sun hath looked upon me." (31)

Hypocrisy is the homage that vice and wrong pay to virtue and justice. It is Satan attempting to clothe himself in the angelic vesture of light. It is equally detestable in morals, politics and religion, in the man and in the nation. To do justice under the pretense of equity and fairness, to reprove vice in public and commit it in private, to pretend to charitable opinion and censoriously condemn, to profess the principles of Masonic beneficence, and close the ear to the wail of distress and the cry of suffering; to eulogize the intelligence of the people, and plot to deceive and betray them by means of their ignorance and simplicty; to prate of purity, and peculate; of honor and basely abandon a sinking cause; of disinterest, and sell one's vote for place and power—are hypocrisies as common as they are infamous and disgraceful. (32)

In reply to Tisdall's vile and unmasonic attack, Grand Master Clark wrote:

"First, this learned writer, Brother F. G. Tisdall, 33⁰, says: *Pomeroy's Democrat*, in all its parts is a white man's paper,' we reply that it would have been better had he said that it was a whited sepulchre full of dead men's bones, the fruits of its labors in defense of treason during our terrible rebellion. Now, for a white man's paper to attack a colored man, and then refuse him a hearing, is base and cowardly. Again, he says: 'So far as its Masonic department is concerned, an organ of legitimate Masonry, we declined to publish the communication referred to as coming from a clandestine source, and returned the same to the writer! This is untrue, as the manuscript was never returned.

"Second. For a legitimate Mason to attack one that he holds to be illegitimate, is unmasonic, and does not accord with that ancient precept that a silent tongue teaches. I pass to the next proposition. He says: 'They have, so far as symbolic Masonry is concerned, Lodges, Grand Lodges and a National Grand Lodge.' Now, this being admitted by my learned brother, F. G. Tisdall, 33⁰, this is all that is in this controversy, for the Lodge I organized at Natchez, under my dispensation, was a blue lodge, purely symbolic with power and authority to make Masons according to the ancient rules and regulations as set forth in the ancient constitution, and not otherwise. But this confession or admission of our learned brother, does not accord with his assertion in his reply to his correspondent 'E. G. De L   ,' in his 29th of March article, headed 'Negroes trying to REVEL as Masons in Mississippi,' this learned 33⁰ says 'This man Clark is a bastard, spurious, illegitimate Mason, and has, as our correspondent was inclined to believe, lied. There does not exist a Lodge of Masons composed of 'American citizens of African descent, in the United or the 'untied' States.'

"Now, I ask the question, does this show that the man Clark has lied, or does it prove that the man Tisdall has lied? Certainly Bro. Tisdall lied when he said in his 29th of March article, that 'there was not a Lodge of Masons composed of 'American citizens of African descent,' in the United or the 'untied' States,' for in his article of the 26th of August, five months later, he says, 'So far as Symbolic Masonry is concerned, they have Lodges, Grand Lodges, and a National Grand Lodge.' Now, this is true and of course the other is untrue, and the man Tisdall, and all who read his two articles, must incline to the belief that he has and did lie.

"I now pass to notice a question of more importance, viz: the legitimacy of Masonry among colored men in the United States of North America. Now, as our learned brother Tisdall has published the Warrant of constitution, verbatim, on which Masonry among colored men in the United States exist, which was granted by the Grand Lodge of England, in 1784 and 1787, Warrant No. 459. 'To our beloved Brethren, Prince Hall, Boston Smith, Thomas Sanderson, and several others.' Thus so far as a Warrant of constitution being granted by the Grand Lodge of England to the above mentioned brethren, constituting them into a regular Lodge of F.A.A.A.Y. Masons, empowering them to make Masons according to ancient rules and regulations, as warranted by the ancient constitution.

"All this being conceded by Brother Tisdall, and admitted by all, we will now notice his criticisms, which are false in theory and in practice to all the principles in Masonry. Our learned brother says: 'The basis upon which the negroes have raised their superstructure, according to the laws which prevail among Masons, especially in the United States, is fatally defective, and their work consequently illegitimate.' My reply to our learned Brother is, that is the very basis upon which our superstructure was raised, viz: Warrant 459, granted by the Grand Lodge of England, in 1784 and 1787, to ole African Lodge, Boston, Massachusetts. And upon this basis we stand and vow, in the language of Walter Scott's Chieftain, who planted his feet firmly on the eternal granite of his native hills, and fixing his revengeful eyes upon his mortal foe, exclaimed in a voice of thunder,

"Come one, come all, this rock shall fly
From its firm base as soon as I."

"So let us invest ourselves with this deep toned spirit of opposition to all and any encroachments, and the basis upon which our Masonic temple stands, and we have nothing to fear. But, says brother Tisdall, 'In the first place, the Grand Lodge of England had no right, in 1784, to establish a Lodge in Boston, as there was a Grand Lodge exercising authority, established there for the State of Massachusetts. In the second place, the Warrant granted in 1784 to the negroes, gave them no authority to establish a Grand Lodge, or a National Grand Lodge, it being nothing more than an ordinary Lodge Warrant. Thirdly, the Warrant, from want of compliance with its provisions, even if it had been legally granted, became forfeited from its failure to make annual returns, and has long since been expunged from the roll of the English Lodges. Their recognition, therefore, would be an outrage on Masonic law and usage, and if they are visited here by persons claiming to be regular Masons it is at the expense of their most solemn covenants.'

"In reply to the first proposition, we say the Grand Lodge of England had a perfect and unequivocal right to grant Warrant No. 459, to African Grand Lodge in 1784 and 1787, as there was no Masonic law or dogma in Masonry anywhere in the world at that time, prohibiting it, and the learned 33⁰ ought to have known that there was another Grand Lodge in Massachusetts at the same time, viz., St. John's Grand Lodge, which was chartered in 1733, thirty-six years before the Grand Lodge of Massachusetts, which was not chartered till the year 1769.

"Now, why has our learned brother singled out the Grand Lodge of Massachusetts? For if the Grand Lodge of England had no right to grant the African Grand Lodge Warrant because of the Grand Lodge of Massachusetts, which was created in 1769, eighteen years before, then certainly she had no right to have granted the Grand Lodge of Massachusetts a Warrant, because St. John's Grand Lodge was chartered in 1733, thirty-six years before. The Grand Lodge of Massachusetts was organized in 1769. Was it an irregular and clandestine body because organized thirty-six years after St. John's Grand Lodge? It was never so regarded. Both were located in Boston, and each treated the other as an equal in the union of the two in 1792. History relates no disturbance between them on the question of Jurisdiction. If the charter of 1784 was 'irregular' because of the jurisdiction of the charter of 1769, why was not the charter of 1769 equally 'irregular' because of the charter of 1733? Or did the fact that one was issued to the white man and the other to the black, make the difference? And if so, where is the Masonic law making the distinction in color? The truth is, that the dogma of a Grand Lodge possessing exclusive jurisdiction in a State or Territory where located, much less in a whole continent, is preposterous and is a comparatively new one, purely of American origin, and is not today acknowledged by Grand Lodges anywhere except in the United States.

"This dogma was first enunciated at the union of the two Grand Lodges in Massachusetts, in 1792, and we believe for the criminal and unmasonic purpose of excluding the African Grand Lodge from the rights and benefits of Masonry in this country, which has signally failed, and in the language of that truly learned and high-minded Masonic jurist, A. T. C. Pierson, in his exposition of Masonry among colored Men in this country, which we have learned so much from, and quoted so often, says, 'But as there was no such law, even in America, and no such claims had been made in 1784 or 1787, and not until five years afterwards, the granting of a charter to African Grand Lodge was not a violation of the jurisdictional rights of the Grand Lodge of Massachusetts, or either of them, and hence was not a clandestine body!'

"This is true, and so acknowledged everywhere among Masons except where innovation has made a lie.

"But we pass to notice brother Tisdall's last proposition, viz: that 'the warrant was but an ordinary Warrant and for want of compliance with its provisions, became forfeited and was expunged from the roll of English Lodges.'

"In reply we say that the Warrant of African Grand Lodge was the same as that of the Grand Lodge of St. John's and the Grand Lodge of Massachusetts, with equal jurisdictional authority and power, and if one was but an ordinary Warrant, then was the other two, if the two had the right to assume the rights of a Grand Lodge from the ordinary Warrant, why not the other? Second. If the one was expunged from the rolls of English Lodges for non-compliance of the charter, why not the other two? These two Lodges ceased, not only to make returns, but to work, for a number of years, then from their scattered and defunct masses, ogranized without the knowledge or authority of their superior, and proceeded to what is now their status all over this country. Now, if brother Tisdall's theory is true, then is Masonry fatally defective, irregular and clandestine, all over this country among the American Lodges, white or colored, and especially among the white Lodges. But we hold that his theory is false and untrue, and affirm the doctrine that Masons in their constitutional numbers had the right to organize and form Lodges and Grand Lodges, as they did, both white and colored, except the false and unmasonic American dogma, viz: That a Grand Lodge has the exclusive right to the exclusion of all others.

"We quote brother Tisdall's last proposition as follows: 'These colored brudders have, on more occasion than one, in years gone by, published their list of dignitaries in the columns of the press, and probably with the desire to receiving the benefits of our quarter of a million circulation, this year honored us with their notice, but though highly sensible of the intended honor, we most respectfully declined to be the medium of communication between them and the regular constituted Fraternity.'

"In reply to this last proposition of our learned and would be jurist, Tisdall, 33^0, is that whether we did or did not desire the benefit of a notice before his quarter of a million readers, we certainly got it in as much as he published the Warrant, verbatim, as granted by the Grand Lodge of England to the African Grand Lodge, from which our right and legitimacy hails. I think he has done more to enlighten his quarter of a million readers than his foolish and unwise criticism of its legitimacy or the right of the Grand Lodge of England to grant it, and in doing this he has done what he says he positively declinded to do, viz: 'the medium of communication' between the regular fraternities in the United States. Now, in disposing of brother Tisdall and his criticism, we do it with no ill will of heart, but with a sincere prayer to God that he may on due reflection over the many true Masonic lessons he has so often learned while worshipping at the shrine of our beloved order, be constrained to return to the devine attribute, truth." (33)

And with that, Grand Master Alexander Clark closed the books on a most shameful chapter of American Masonry. The black scholar-historian and Prince Hall Freemason, Bro. W. E. B. DuBois wrote:

"...somebody in each era must make clear the facts with utter disregard to his own wish and desire and belief. What we have got to know, as far as possible, are the things that actually happened in the world... the historian has no right, posing as scientist, to conceal or distort facts; and until we distinguish between these two functions of the chronicler of human action we are going to render it easy for a muddled world out of sheer ignorance to make the same mistake ten times over." (34)

And this writer has attempted to reconstruct events and reactions, accurately and honestly. Masonically, this has not been a kind story, but one that had to be told. The facts are there for all to see, as they were recorded so many years ago. Is it not true that regardless of how small or insignificant an incident may appear, or how buried it may lay in the history books, some one, some day may very well come along and expose it before the entire world, and the world will pass their judgment on it!

In 1858, before the "Niggerdom in Regalia" incident, before there was a Lodge named for him and before he became the first black United States Senator, Bro. Hiram Rhodes Revels would record:

> "We so far, with such historical data as we at present can reach, can see no essential difference between the course of our colored Lodges and the primary American Grand Lodges of our pale brethren. If, therefore, they cannot affiliate with us, we beg of them not hastily to condemn us. We feel that whilst they condemn us, they must condemn themselves, to a great degree. We believe, too, that in time a spirit less marked by prejudice will prevail toward us, which we hope to merit and to earn by a close adherence to the ancient pattern of most honorable Masons, and by our personal efforts to improve in all the moral and social qualities so ennobling to human nature." (35)

How ironic it is, that the rabid negrophobe Confederate General Albert Pike, who is quoted often in this work, who swore he would leave Masonry before he would accept a black man as a Freemason, would be publishing his famed *Morals and Dogmas*, also in 1871, and would write:

> "There can be no genuine Brotherhood without mutual regard, good opinion and esteem, mutual charity, and mutual allowance for faults and failings. It is those only who learn habitually to think better of each other, and expect, allow for, and overlook the evil, who can be Brethren one of the other, in any true sense of the word. Those who gloat over the failings of one another, who think each other to be naturally base and low, of a nature in which the evil predominates and excellence is not to be looked for, cannot be even friends, and much less Brethren. No one can have a right to think meanly of his race, unless he also thinks meanly of himself. If, from a single fault or error, he judges of the character of another, and takes the single act as evidence of the whole nature of the man and the whole course of his life, he ought to consent to be judged by the same rule, and to admit it to be right that others should thus uncharitably condemn himself." (36)

Today, as a monument to the Masonic ideals of Alexander Clark stands H. R. Revels Lodge No. 3 F. & A.M. in Natchez, Mississippi.

Alexander Clark, Grand Master Prince Hall Grand Lodge of Missouri.

Members of the 41st and 42nd Congress of the United States—
Standing are Representatives Robert C. De Large of South Carolina
and Jefferson H. Long of Georgia. Sitting from left to right: Senator
of the United States H. R. Revels of Mississippi and four other
Representatives: Benjamin S. Turner of Alabama, Josiah T. Walls of
Florida, Joseph H. Rainey and R. Brown Elliott, the second Grand
Master of the P.H.G.L. of South Carolina.

Rev. Thomas W. Stringer—
First Grand Master of Ohio,
First Grand Master of Mississippi.

REFERENCE TO PART VI

1. Harry A. Williamson, *Men of Mark in Prince Hall Freemasonry*, read June 24, 1943, *PHLORONY* Transactions of the Prince Hall Lodge of Research of New York, Vol. 1, 1943, p. 30.

2. Alexander Clark, M. W. Grand Masters Address, Proceedings of the M. W. Grand Lodge of Missouri, Sixth Annual Communication, Keokuk, Iowa, July 1st, 1872, p. 10.

3. *The Corner Stone* (New York, Saturday, Dec. 8, 1878).

4. W. G. Sibley, *The Story of Freemasonry*, Gallipolis, Ohio, The Lions Paw Club, 1904, p. 72.

5. W. E. Burghardt Du Bois, *Black Reconstruction*, Philadelphia, Pa., Albert Saifer: Publisher, 1935, Chapter xi, p. 434.

6. Fifty-Second Grand Annual Communication, Grand Lodge of Mississippi A. F. & A. M., Jackson, Mississippi, Jan. 1870, Thos. B. Gathright Grand Master.

7. Fifty-Third Grand Annual Communication, Grand Lodge of Mississippi, A. F. & A. M., Vicksburg, Mississippi, Jan. 1871.

8. William R. Denslow, *10,000 Famous Freemasons*, Transactions, Missouri Lodge of Research, 1957, p. 291. "He was not a Mason, although his father and Brother were."

9. Charles H. Wesley, *The History of the Prince Hall Grand Lodge of Ohio 1849-1960*, Wilberforce, Ohio, Central State Press, 1961, p. 91-92.

10. Peter M. Bergman, *The Chronological History of the Negro in America*, New York, Harper & Row, 1969, p. 263.

11. Proceedings of the Most Worshipful Prince Hall Grand Lodge of Missouri F. & A. M., 1866.

12. *Ibid.*

13. *Ibid.*

14. *Ibid.*

15. *Ibid.*

16. *Ibid.*

17. *Ibid.*

18. Proceedings of the Most Worshipful Prince Hall Grand Lodge of Missouri 1870, p. 16.

19. *Ibid*, p. 14.

20. Proceedings of the Most Worshipful Prince Hall Grand Lodge of Missouri F. & A. M., 1872, p. 18.

21. Proceedings of the Grand Lodge of Mississippi A. F. & A. M., Fifty-Eighth Annual Communication, returns of subordinate Lodges—1869, p. 65.

22. Denslow, *op. cit.*, p. 63.

23. Proceedings of the Grand Lodge of Mississippi A. F. & A. M., Fifty-Ninth Annual Communication, 1870, p. 19.

24. *The Corner Stone*, New York, Saturday, Dec. 8, 1878.

25. H. L. Haywood, *Famous Masons and Masonic Presidents*, Richmond, Virginia, Macoy, 1944, p. 26.

26. F. G. Tisdall, *The Objects, Antiquity and Universality of Masonry*, an address delivered in St. John's Lodge No. 1, New York, February 28, 1850 by Right Worshipful F. G. Tisdall, Master of said Lodge.

27. *Ibid.*

28. Albert Pike, *Morals and Dogma* of the Ancient and Accepted Scottish Rite of Freemasonry, 1871.

29. Proceedings of Prince Hall Grand Lodge of Missouri, 1872, p. 19-21.

30. Pike, *op. cit.*

31. *The Song of Solomon*, Books of the Old Testament.

32. Pike, *op. cit.*, p. 73.

33. Proceedings of Prince Hall Grand Lodge of Missouri, 1872, p. 21-26.

34. Du Bois, *op. cit.*, p. 722.

35. H. R. Revels, An Address delivered to the members of Prince Hall Lodge No. 10 F. & A. M., St. Louis, Missouri, January 28, 1858.

36. Pike, *op. cit.*, p. 856-857.

VII

JOSEPH G. FINDEL—
HONORARY PRINCE HALL GRAND MASTER

Within the pages of Prince Hall Masonic history, there is no more interesting a figure than the famed German Masonic writer and scholar, Joseph Gottfried Findel (1828-1905).

As a writer he was mainly noted for his *General History of Freemasonry*, which was published in 1861 and translated into English in 1865 and 1866. (1) This work was the forerunner of Robert Freke Gould's great *History of Freemasonry*, published in three volumes from 1882 to 1887.(2)

Bro. Findel was initiated in Lodge Eleusis Zur Vershwiegenheit at Bayreuth on October 19, 1856. He founded the Union of German Freemasons in 1860 and was the editor of an interesting Masonic journal at Leipzig in 1858, entitled *Craft Lodge*. In 1874 he published *Genius and Form of Freemasonry*.

It was Bro. Findel's *History of Freemasonry* (3) that came to the attention of the Grand Master of Prince Hall Masons in Massachusetts, that fire-brand, the very remarkable Lewis Hayden who noted in the appendix of his pamphlet, *War of Races*, (4) that "speaking of the Lodges of Colored people which worked separately," Bro. Findel says, "it was long doubted whether these were legally constituted until Brother Dr. R. Barthelmess, of Brooklyn, demonstrated that such was the case, so that their recognition can no longer, with any show of reason, be withheld." (5)

During the period, it was evident to the Prince Hall Masonic Grand Lodges across the country that the Caucasian Grand Lodges in the United States would neither recognize them nor acknowledge them as Masons, even though they had in their possession a Charter from the Mother Grand Lodge of England.

Realizing that they could expect only racism from their American counterparts, who devised as a convenient weapon against Prince Hall Masonry the so-called doctrine of exclusive Grand Lodge jurisdiction, which even the Masonic scholar (who is classed by Prince Hall Masonry as a racist) General Albert Pike declared as a false Masonic law. (6)

The Prince Hall Grand Lodges led by Bro. Justin Holland of Ohio, (7) and the Grand Lodges of Missouri, New York and Massachusetts, began to seek Masonic recognition abroad, and within a short time, fraternal recognition was accorded them from six foreign Masonic powers, the German Grand Lodge League representing eight Grand bodies, France, Italy, Hungary, Peru and the Dominican Republic. (8)

While the debate concerning Prince Hall Masonry was raging in European Masonic circles, American Caucasian jurisdictions protested vigorously against any recognition of their Black countrymen, but found themselves often in a rather precarious position when distinguished French and German Masons, Caubet, Grimaux, Dr. Barthelmess and Bro. Findel began to test their Grand Lodge regularity, and found them not as regular as they had claimed. (9)

In 1870 Grand Master Lewis Hayden and the Prince Hall Grand Lodge of Massachusetts issued the following resolution in the form of a certificate:

WHEREAS, from the beginning of our Masonic existence, we knew of no Historian, in Europe or America, who has made mention of our being an organized body of Masons, except in a disparaging manner, until *Bro. J. G. Findel* published his inestimable *"History of Freemasonry,"* in which we find a different spirit toward us, that of "Truth," characterized by "Brotherly Love," expressed in the following words, "It was long doubted whether these were legally constituted, until Brother Doctor R. Barthelmess, of Brooklyn, demonstrated from the history of their first beginning, that such was the case, so that their recognition can no longer, with any show of reason, be withheld."

AND WHEREAS, true to the above expressions, he stands today vindicating our cause in his own glorious and triumphing Fatherland, the champion of truth and justice in the endeavor to establish our disputed Masonic claim before the civilized nations of the earth:

NOW THEREFORE, BE IT RESOLVED, that he be, and is hereby, elected a Life Member of the M. W. Prince Hall G. L. of the State of Massachusetts, with the rank and title of "Honorary Grand Master."

RESOLVED, FURTHER, that the proper documents be forwarded to him under the Seal of this Grand Lodge and that the Grand Secretary transmit to his address copies of these resolutions and proceedings.

Done in Boston, Massachusetts, this 25th day of August, A.D. 1870, A.L. 5870, and in the 86th year of our Masonic Existence.

LEWIS HAYDEN, Grand Master

The Collar, Apron, Jewels and Gauntlets of an Honorary Grand Master were sent to Bro. Findel, and Grand Master Lewis Hayden, himself author of a number of pamphlets, dedicated his famous *Masonry Among Colored Men in Massachusetts* (10) to this dedicated German Masonic scholar and Mason, and began with the famous lines:

"My Dear Sir and Brother: As we read of the struggle of our fathers against the oppressions brought to bear upon them, previous to and since the commencement of our government, to dispossess them of what manhood they possessed, we find that they had to struggle to maintain even the smallest claim to humanity, so that none need be surprised that, after having refused them the means of education, of which Prince Hall complained in an address delivered before our Lodge in 1792, nay, more, in parts of the country the education of our people was absolutely forbidden, by laws the spirit of which can be seen by reference to the action of the house of delegates of Virginia, and which expressed the American sentiment of that day they sought to extract, by a system of laws, even the power of reason, as the following shows: 'We have, as far as possible, closed every avenue by which light might enter their [the slaves'] minds. If we could extinguish the capacity to see the light, our work would be complete and we would be safe."

"No one will question the fact that the Masonic fraternity was represented by the men who passed such laws as those alluded to, the baneful effects of which we are contending against to this day. For the old adage is literally true, 'that those we wrong, we hate.' They have wronged us and our fathers; hence they hate us. And were they the same men in their Lodges they have shown themselves to be in their several legislative halls, I repeat that none need be surprised to find that in the organization of their Lodges and Grand Lodges have they persistently rejected the colored Mason, regardless of their claim as man and Masons. And to do so, they have resorted to all kinds of subterfuges, ignoring truth, landmarks, and usuage; all have been thrown to the wind." (11)

Bro. Findel proved himself a dedicated fighter for recognition of Prince Hall Masonry on the shores of Europe, and his eloquence was equal to that of Grand Master Hayden.

"After I had already demanded, ten years ago, the recognition of the Colored Grand Lodges as a matter of justice and fraternity, and as a Masonic duty, by order of the Just and Perfect Prince Hall Grand Lodge, in Boston, I addressed some time ago the request to the German Grand Lodge to be recognized and eventually get into closer brotherly connection with them. Now, the Grand

Lodge of the Eclectic Union, Frankfurt, on the Maine, which, in the so-called
Jews' question, was ahead of all in decidedly maintaining the correct Masonic
ground, was also the first to officially congratulate me upon my appointment as
an honorary Grand Master, and to unreservedly declare in favor of recognizing
my constituents. From the nine German Grand Lodges, the Grand Lodges of
Hungary approved of getting into closer connection by mutual representation.
The Grand Lodge of 'Zur Sonne' in Bayreuth, had actually recognized the colored Grand Lodges of American before by allowing its filial Lodge in Karlsruhe
to issue circulars to them, and by receiving from them and receipting contributions for Strasburg and Kehl. It would be an outrage at once revolting and
demoralizing to assess on Colored Lodges contributions for Masonic purposes,
and afterwards deprive these colored brethren and Lodges of their charter as
Masons, and shut them out from the Lodges. He, who knows the delicacy of sentiment and the noblesse of our Bro. Van Cornburg, will not doubt for a moment
that he and with him his Lodge mean to resolutely come forward in the defense
of the colored brethren. But by this very acceptance of money contributions,
and the thanks tendered to the colored brethren, especially those of Ohio, for
their brotherly advances, have not only the brethren in Karlsruhe, Kehl and
Strasburg, not only the Grand Lodge 'Zur Sonne,' but all German Masons have
taken upon themselves a debt of honor from which they can never withdraw.
The Grand Lodge of Hamburg being, as a matter of course, in the very beginning, in favor of recognition, did not want to take the lead in this affair, exposed,
as it already is, to the hatred of the American Grand Lodges. The Grand Lodge
Royal York in Friendship, at Berlin, in declining to enter into closer connection,
has expressly recognized the Prince Hall Grand Lodge as being just and perfect.
In the Grand Lodge of Saxony further inquiries were to be made before definitely adopting a resolution. The whole affair, however, was finally brought before
the forum of the Union of German Grand Lodges, which will not make a
definite decision before next year. Bro. Van Mensch, representative of the
Grand Lodge of New York, has already tried to exert his influence in the last session, by the following document, addressed to the late Bro. Warnatz:

"M.. W.. Grand Master: Animated by the desire to contribute, as much as is
within me, to the maintaining of the friendly relations fortunately existing, with
but a solitary exception, between the Most Worshipful German and North
American Grand Lodges, and in view of the German Grand Master's Convention, which is soon to meet, I have the honor of asking your attention to an offer
which the alleged honorary Grand Master and representative-in-chief of the colored so-called Prince Hall Grand Lodge, at Boston, Massachusetts, Bro. Findel,
at Leipsic, has, in assurance of which offer is to bring about a closer connection
between them and his constituents. I beg leave, M.. W.. Grand Master, to
respectfully call to your mind the resolution and motion which the Grand Lodge
of Saxony had passed in its session of June 28, 1860—whereby the North
American Colored Lodges and their members are denied, for the present,
recognition as 'just and perfect' Masons. In the Grand Lodge Convention, held
on December 16, 1871,—it was resolved, however, to institute new inquires
about the genuineness of these Lodges, and more fully understand the questions
of the legitimacy of Prince Hall Grand Lodge. The motives which lead the

Grand Lodge to its first resolve, hold good this very day in their full extent, unchanged and unmitigated, and since June 28, 1860, when the above-mentioned resolution was passed, no new argument could be advanced to show that the Prince Hall Grand Lodge was legally constituted and established just and perfect.

"Such valid evidence, which cannot be furnished however, must necessarily be placed in the hands of the German Grand Lodge Association which is soon to meet, and to which, according to the Constitution, is reserved the task of examining into and deciding upon this point, before this could be decided upon the regularity and the recognition of Prince Hall Grand Lodge, which it is well known, is disputed by the Grand Lodge of Massachusetts next interested in it, and by all the other Grand Lodges of the United States.

"The only supposed proof in evidence [is that] which Brother Dr. Barthelmess of Brooklyn put in, to found the legitimacy of Prince Hall Grand Lodge, is the Charter, the constitutional patent of the year 1784, of the Grand Lodge of England, for the Colored African St. John's Lodge, No. 458, at Boston.

"In regard to that charter, it is to be remarked, however, that it extinguished itself on account of non-use. The Lodge soon after its establishment had failed to report to the Mother Grand Lodge, and did not meet for a number of years. The said Mother Grand Lodge of England, soon afterwards, as will be seen from its correspondence, struck the name of the Lodge from the register of its Daughter Lodges, and the returned charter has never been renewed.

"The African Lodge therefore had no longer a legitimate existence. Of said charter a copy has been retained in Boston, and this illegal copy conserved in the archives of Prince Hall Grand Lodge, and not the original document, form the basis upon which some persons started anew the extinct Lodge. Out of this irregular Lodge, and two other St. John Lodges in Providence and Philadelphia, whose rightful establishment is nowhere proven, the Colored Prince Hall Grand Lodge in Boston has sprung, from which all other Negro Lodges and Grand Lodges in the United States of North America, deduce their origin and authority.

"All these, and other corroborating circumstances are well known to the German Grand Lodges from the various publications of the Grand Lodges of Massachusetts and New York, and need not here be enlarged upon, as there has never any attempt been made to refute them.

"But supposing the case that the Colored Lodges in the United States were originally just and perfect Lodges of Free Masons, which decidedly is not admitted, even then their recognition on the part of the German Grand Lodges would violate the principle of the Masonic law of the United States. The Grand Lodges in the United States claim for themselves the exclusive right of jurisdiction within their own territory, and grant the same to foreign Grand Lodges. The inference is that the 'African Lodge,' constituted by the Grand Lodge of England, long after the establishment of the legitimate and generally acknowledged Grand Lodge of Massachusetts, would not have had a lawful existence even if its members should not have been negroes.

"Furthermore an agreement between all the Grand Lodges in the United

"Furthermore an agreement between all the Grand Lodges in the United States, is now enforced as a law, viz: that in every State of the Union there can in but one Grand Lodge lawfully exist, which, being sovereign and independent its jurisdiction possesses within its well defined territory, the sole right of establishing Lodges and of exercising full authority and control over all Lodges of symbolic Masonry in their respective States. In consideration of this fact alone even if Prince Hall Grand Lodge could lay claim to legitimate existence, the alternative would arise for the German Grand Lodge Association to either keep up good relations with the, so to say, white Grand Lodges of the United States, or to forfeit them, when said Association should be determined to recognize the colored Freemasons' Grand Lodge of Massachusetts, and some others of like caste.

"The Most Worshipful Grand Lodge, which I have the honor of representing near the M.. W.. Grand Lodge Association, by recognizing, not 'just and perfect' Grand Lodges and Lodges, and by disregarding the legal institutions in the American Lodge affairs, will bring about a rupture with the sister Grand Lodges in the United States, and connected them will deprive numerous German Freemasons temporarily staying there, and settling, of the opportunity and the benefit of visiting the American Lodges, and associating with their brethren there, and of claiming their counsel, and in case of necessity their assistance and helpful aid. In order not to appear in the light of silently working for the resolutions of the German Grand Lodge Association, at variance perhaps, with the above presuppositions and to escape every responsibility, I, in behalf of my M.W. constituents, the Grand Lodge of the State of New York, beg leave to most respectfully and request:

"The M.. W.. Grand Master to inform the esteemed members of the German Grand Lodge Association at their next meeting, of the contents of this communication, to invite their consideration of this subject and to kindly bring their influence to bear upon a decision in favor of the German and North American Grand Lodges and Freemasonry in general.

"Knowing that Freemasonry finds its purest expression, its support and firm hold, especially in the German, English and North American Grand Lodges, we had to deeply regret in more than one sense, any disturbance of the cordiality between two of these main groups, for which, moreover, in Germany, a practical motive is not given at all. With greatest reverence, I am,

M.. W.. Grand Master,
Dresden, May 12, 1872

Your truly allied and devoted brother,
Von Mensch,
Rep. of the M.. W.. Grand Lodge of the State of New York."

Bro. Von Mensch did not go to the trouble of inquiring into and getting acquainted with the circumstances, materials and facts of the case, else he could have never made such awkward and untenable statements.

There is nothing easier than to refute him point by point.

First, it is quite an unworthy imposition to the union of German Grand Lodges if Bro. Von Mensch refers to the benefit of being able to attend

American Lodges, and to solicit the counsel and support of American brethren, thereby putting down purely external advantages and enjoyments as a motive for the Grand Master's verdict. Such feeble arguments will hardly have any weight with us, for our German brethren as a rule are little edified by the American Grand Lodges and can, if most of the Grand Lodges had their ban upon us, attend the three Hamburg (German) and the colored Lodges. (12)

Not much better is his referring to the exclusive right of territorial jurisdiction asserted by the American Grand Lodges which is founded on the Monroe doctrine, but not on the general right of Masons, and is partly a prejudice and partly an injustice. In Berlin there are three Grand Lodges working side-by-side, in Paris two, and in former times there were two in London and two in New York. How can the American Grand Lodges claim the exclusive right of jurisdiction in view of the colored Grand Lodges, which now accepted by them, but suppressed, were by force of inexorable necessity compelled to start Lodges and Grand Lodges of their own, that with some exceptions have been longer in existence there than most of the white Lodges. Here is not an acknowledged absolute theory to be upheld, but facts and historical rights are to be considered. We Free Masons recognize no difference of color or race and we hold the Grand Lodges of the white and colored men equally entitled to recognition. Still more, there is a duty of humanity which we have to fulfill to the colored men, to recognize them; means to elevate them intellectually and morally, to benefit them and to eminently act like a Mason. To recognize them and to enter into intellectual communication and brotherly intercourse with them, is not only our, but principally the American Mason's duty and if they from a hatred and prejudice against the race rid themselves of this duty, then, surely it would be not incumbent upon the union of German Grand Lodges to act alike. In honor of the American brotherhood be it gladly acknowledged that they have already been infused with a sense of their duty, the consciousness of which is gaining headway in their own ranks, and in carrying it out, they are only delayed by the sick ally of the Constitution of Grand Lodges.

If Prince Hall Grand Lodge and the colored Lodges are being recognized in Germany, the American masonic crisis will be salubriously accelerated, and the triumph of the idea so much sooner achieved. What Bro. Von Mensch demands is a greater regard on the part of the German Grand Lodges for the American Lodges than is bestowed upon the Hamburg Grand Lodge allied with them, which, as is well known, has already been exonerated from a lack of cordiality.

The main point: Bro. Von Mensch admits himself that the Mother Lodge of the colored Lodges, and the Prince Hall Grand Lodge, the African Lodge at Boston, has been regularly constituted by the Grand Lodge of England, and has been a *just* and *perfect* Lodge; but what he further adds in order to dispute its legality, is entirely untrue. The Lodge *did not stop* soon after its establishment to report to the Mother Grand Lodge, for in the year 1792, Bro. Prince Hall was still connected with the English Grand Lodge; and its Grand Secretary, Bro. W. White, wrote on August, 1792, as follows: 'Very much obliged to you for the news about your Lodge, (African). I sincerely wish you every success, and should consider myself happy if I could contribute anything to that end. Enclosed please find the calender.—[*Vide* the Address of W. S. Gardener, Grand Master of the white Grand Lodge of Massachusetts, p. 100. 1872.]

Furthermore, it is not true that after the Grand Lodge of England struck the name of African Lodge from the register of its daughter Lodges, for the striking was not done, as the present Grand Secretary of the Grand Lodge of England testifies, before the year 1813, when all American Lodges then still on record, were wiped from the register. It is not true that the Charter was returned to the Grand Lodge, or extinguished by non-use, for the Lodge is up to this date in possession of the original, (not a copy) and had then as much a footing of its own, and enjoyed as much independence, as did the German and all the American Lodges. But even if the legal origin of the colored Grand Lodges should be wrapped in doubt—which is not so, however—would that furnish a reason to deny them the deserved recognition? Never! For they work according to Masonic rite and Masonic principles, and in the same Masonic spirit as we do; and there is no one in Germany to whom it ever occurred to dispute the legality of Gr. L. L. v. D. Swedish systems, although it derived its constitutions not from a recognized Grand Lodge, but from the still isolated "Eckleff" Lodge, although its acts did not correspond with the Masonic principle, and although it did not wait for the necessary twelve Lodges before it started. Nobody hesitated to recognize the Grand Lodge of Hamburg, because it owes its existence not to any Grand Lodge; nor Hungary, though it owes existence not to any Grand Lodge, but to the "John's Lodge," to the unity in the country founded by Bro. Lewis, and based upon his dubious Scottish privileges.

Looking aside from other Grand Lodges and further instances, and especially the (White) Grand Lodge of Massachusetts, I simply ask upon what footing stand all our German Grand Lodges, if you want to measure them with Bro. Van Mensch's rule, and say their original Constitutions were extinguished by non-use? That is, by falling back on "strict observance," and joining in all peculiar to that time. What legal existence have in the sense of Bro. Van Mensch—the Grand Lodges of Italy, the Grand Orient of France, the Supreme Grand Council of the 33⁰, with all their Constitutions? Enough: The Prince Hall Grand Lodge, both from a material and formal point of law, is not inferior to any other Grand Lodge in the world; and there is not a shade of authority for refusing to recognize it. It would be sad, disgraceful, and a bad omen, if in this just cause the union of German Grand Lodges should pass a resolution in the negative. Quod Deus avertat. (13)

All of the Masonic regalia presented to Bro. Findel by Grand Master Lewis Hayden and the Prince Hall Grand Lodge of Massachusetts were placed on exhibition in the Masonic Museum of the Grand Lodge Zur Sonne (The Sun) in Bayreuth, in Bavaria. But when Adolph Hitler came to power he destroyed or desecrated every Masonic edifice in Germany. The Museum of the Grand Lodge Zur Sonne did not escape his wrath. The only items remaining today are the Grand Master Jewels which were presented to Bro. Findel.

In a recent letter to this writer, the curator of the German Masonic Museum in Bayreuth wrote:

Bayreuth, Dec. 10, 1975

The Honorary (Grand Master's) Jewels which Brother Grand Master R. W. Findel has received from the Prince Hall Grand Lodge of Massachusetts, and of which you have pictures, is [sic] exhibited at the "Deutsches Freimaurer Museum" in Bayreuth.

On July 12, 1970 (Prince Hall) Military Lodge No. 140 with 107 people and on August 27, 1972, Lodge No. 144 with 25 members have [sic] visited our museum.

From the first Lodge we received a large engraved plaque and from Lodge No. 144 an engraved dipper. Both pieces are exhibited and a beautiful memory for us.

With Brotherly Greetings,
Henrich Wilhelm Lorenz, 33⁰

And so, a small portion of Prince Hall Masonry is preserved, thousands of miles from the country of Prince Hall, and within the glass case are the jewels of a Grand Master, symbols of the legendary Lewis Hayden and the Prince Hall Grand Lodge of Massachusetts.

They represent the true stature of European Freemasons, Bro. Findel, and others, who were true and just to the spirit of Freemasonry. The jewels represent the struggle of Prince Hall Freemasonry to be accorded its rightful place in the Masonic community. They symbolize the fight against American racism as practiced by the Caucasian Grand Lodges then, as they practice it today, and against the fascism of Hitlerism against Freemasonry in Europe.

And it is symbolic that in this decade that Prince Hall Military Lodges stationed in Germany, would pay their respects to this Museum that holds so many memories of the Prince Hall Masonic past.

Grand Master Lewis Hayden

Bro. J. G. Findel

MASONRY AMONG COLORED MEN IN MASSACHUSETTS.

No. 13
Case
Shelf

TO THE

Right Worshipful

J. G. FINDEL,

HONORARY GRAND MASTER OF THE PRINCE
HALL GRAND LODGE,

AND

GENERAL REPRESENTATIVE THEREOF TO THE LODGES
UPON THE CONTINENT OF EUROPE.

BOSTON:
PUBLISHED BY LEWIS HAYDEN.
1871.

Frontispiece of Hayden's Book

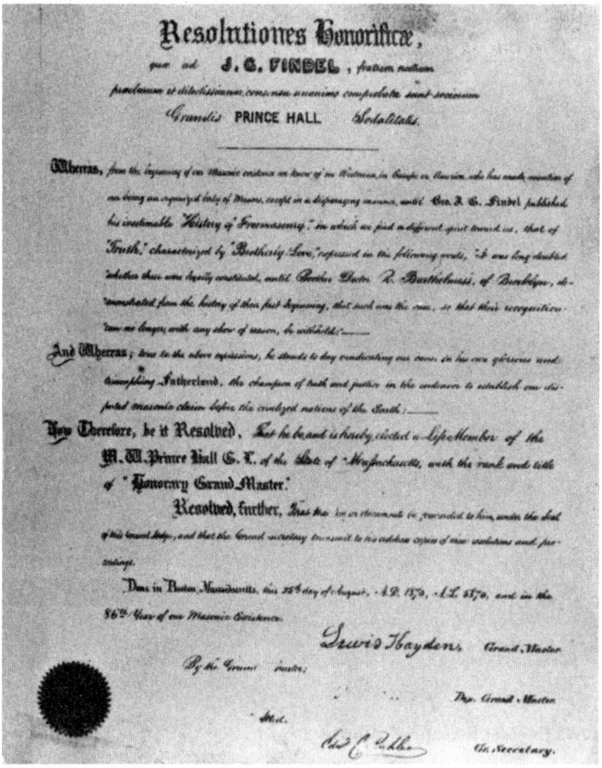

Resolution Certificate Presented to Bro. Findel

Jewels presented to Joseph Gabriel Findel

Prince Hall Military Lodge No. 140 visiting German Masonic Museum with Bro. Lorenz, Curator.

REFERENCE FOR PART VII

1. William R. Denslow, *10,000 Famous Freemasons*, reprinted in the Transactions of the Missouri Lodge of Research (Trenton, Mo., 1958), p. 49.

2. Robert Freke Gould (1836-1915) was a founder of the famous Quatuor Coronati Lodge No. 2076 of London, in 1884. He wrote *The Four Old Lodges* in 1879 and in 1899, *Military Lodges*. His greatest work was his *History of Freemasonry*, published in three volumes from 1882 to 1887. Denslow, *op. cit.*, p. 132-133.

3. Translated from German by Asher & Co., 13 Bedford Street, London, 1866.

4. Lewis Hayden, *Grand Lodge Jurisdictional Claim or War of Races*, an address before the Prince Hall Grand Lodge of Massachusetts, Festival of St. John the Baptist, June 24, 1868, by Lewis Hayden, Grand Master, p. 92.

5. *Ibid*, p. 92.

6. Charles H. Wesley, *The History of the Prince Hall Grand Lodge of the State of Ohio 1849-1960*, Wilberforce, Ohio, Central State College Press, 1961, p. 72, states "In this connection, General Albert Pike on February 7, 1877, sent a letter to the Supreme Council of Peru with the following statement, quoted in Ohio Masonry, 1925: 'The doctrine of exclusive Grand Lodge jurisdiction had grown up in the United States, and has been accepted here as politic and in the interest of harmony. It does not prevail in Europe, and is not a part of Masonic organic law, and its zealots here have not been content to stop when they pushed it to the verge of absurdity.' "

7. Wesley, *op. cit.*, p. 73, "Since foreign Lodges had no such views as American Lodges, correspondence and contacts were kept up by these Lodges. The one Prince Hall Mason most interested was Justin Holland who conducted this work in a most effective manner."

8. Harry E. Davis, *A History of Freemasonry Among Negroes in America* United Supreme Council, A.A.S.R., Northern Jurisdiction, U.S.A., Prince Hall Affiliation, Inc., p. 112-113, states "These recognitions were accorded not only by formal decree of these jurisdictions but by the interchange of representatives between them and Ohio, the reciprocal elections of honorary members, and the conferring of Jewels and other Masonic honors upon these representatives." Wesley, *op. cit.*, p. 80, states "These recognitions were important not only to the Grand Lodge of Ohio but also to Prince Hall Masons generally, for they gave evidence of approval and of brotherhood at a period in history when such sanctions were needed. Prince Hall Masons had been rebuffed as well and were unrecognized by American Masons, while these recognitions had little influence on American attitudes toward Prince Hall Masons, they were of inestimable value in strengthening the morale and giving assurance to Prince Hall Masons that they were upon sound foundations and that segregation and denial of fellowship could not validate their foundations in Masonic history and tradition."

9. Davis, *op. cit.*, p. 114; Lewis Hayden, *Masonry Among Colored Men in Massachusetts*, Masonic Journal, Vol. 1, No. 1, 2 & 3, Moline, Illinois, June 1879.

10. Lewis Hayden published *Caste Among Masons* in 1866; *Grand Lodge Jurisdictional Claim or War of Races* in 1868; and *Masonry Among Colored Men in Massachusetts* in 1871. All of the pamphlets deal with the question of legitimacy, but they contain valuable historical material as well.

11. *Proceedings of the Prince Hall Grand Lodge of Ohio*, 22nd Annual Communication, August 21, 1872, p. 71.

12. Refers to the German Lodges in New York, and the clash between the Grand Lodge of Hamburg and the Caucasian Grand Lodge of New York, considered by this writer as one of the most shameful incidents in Masonic history. The Committee on Foreign Correspondence of the Caucasian Grand Lodge of New York reported concerning the German Lodges in New York under the jurisdiction of the Grand Lodge of Hamburg, "It has now withdrawn or offered to withdraw the Charters of its illegitimate subordinates. Though apprised of the universal sentiment which prevails among the Grand Lodges of United States in condemnation of its acts, it persists in keeping up the Lodges in the Jurisidiction of New York, in violation of our laws and in defiance of our authority. This is not all. It is indeed but a tithe of her offending. It is a venial, and excusable offence in comparison to a much greater which she is seeking now to perpetuate. Because we have declared her two subordinates irregular, and suspended intercourse with her till their Charters are recalled, she has invented a means of reprisal, a mode of retaliation, which for deliberate revenge has no parallel in the history of Masonry... . She the Grand Lodge of Hamburgh is not only to recognize these bodies (Prince Hall) herself as regular and legitimate Lodges and Grand Lodges, but she is trying to persuade the other Grand Lodges of Europe to do the same thing." Lewis Hayden, *Grand Lodge Jurisdictional Claim or War of Races*, Boston. Edward S. Coombs, 1868, p. 63-64.

13. Ohio Proceedings, *op. cit.*, p. 72.

VIII

MARTIN R. DELANY—MILITANT MASTER MASON

When one attempts to write about Martin Robinson Delany, the writer must approach this subject with caution and discretion, and with awe for Delany's irony and contradictions.

Martin E. Delany was a man who lived so many different experiences, that it is often difficult to separate the several phases of this Prince Hall Mason, who was a man of contradictions, ambitions, inconsistency, pessimism, sensibility, irony and greatness.

He was born in Charlestown, Virginia in 1812, the son of free Negroes, Samuel and Pati Delany. His paternal grandfather was a prince of the Mandingo tribe who had been captured in the Niger Valley, sold into slavery, and subsequently brought to America. Delany received something of an education in Pennsylvania, became active in social and educational projects in the Pittsburgh area, studied medicine but settled into dentistry, traveled in the south, started a newspaper, *The Mystery* in Pittsburgh, and was associated with Frederick Douglass in bringing out the famed newspaper *The North Star.* (1)

He returned to the study of medicine, became involved in an emigration scheme in Central America, put his ideas into print in *"The Condition, Elevation, Emigration, and Destiny of the Colored People of the United States Politically Considered."* (1852) all by the time he was forty, (2) and though these many activities would seem to paint a picture of this extraordinary individual, in reality it barely touches the surface of the complexity and make of this Mason of contradictions.

Delany became a fiery spokesman for Black manhood in the years before, during, and after the Civil War. This short, stocky, black militant attended Harvard Medical School until prejudice forced him out. His hatred of racism led him to consider the use of force and Negro resettlement in Africa as solutions to the problems of slavery and discrimination.

He awoke every morning, thankful, he said, that God had made him a black man. He also advocated violence to halt slave catchers. In his 1852 history of *Black Americans* he insisted, "We must make an issue, create an event, and establish a national position for ourselves."(3)

He not only proposed a Black exodus to Africa, but in 1860 explored the continent for a suitable site. (4) Delany is recorded in American military history as the first Black Major in the United States Army, appointed to this rank directly from civilian life by President Lincoln, who called Delany "a most extraordinary and intelligent Black man."(5)

Delany had eleven children, seven of whom lived. In keeping with his personality, he named his offspring after black heroes. The eldest he named Toussaint L'Ouverture, after the first military hero and liberator of Haiti, who drove the powerful armies of Napolean into the sea. The second, Charles Lennox Remond, after the black abolitionist and fellow Prince Hall Mason who, with Delany, recruited for the 54th Massachusetts Infantry, the first Black Regiment from a Northern State during the Civil War with the added distinction of having the first Prince Hall Military Lodge attached to it. The third, Alexander Dumas, from the brilliant author of *The Three Musketeers* and *The Count of Monte-Cristo;* the fourth, Saint Cyprian from one of the greatest primitive bishops of the Christian Church and the name of his Masonic Lodge. The fifth, Faustin Soulouque, after the late Emperor of Haiti; the sixth, Rameses Placido, from the good King of Egypt, "The ever-living Rameses II," and the poet and martyr of freedom to his race on the Island of Cuba. The seventh, a daughter, Ethiopia Halle Amelia, the country of a race, to which is given the unequalled promise that "she should soon stretch forth her hands unto God." (6)

In 1850 the Federal Fugitive Slave Law was signed into law. It allowed any claimants of a runaway slave to take possession of a Black upon establishing proof of ownership before a Federal Commissioner. No safeguards, such as a jury trial or judicial hearing for the captive, were included. The act provided fines of $1,000 and imprisonment for six months of citizens or officials who failed to aid in the capture of fugitives. Southerners thought that this tough measure would be sufficient to halt the escape of their slaves.

Grand Master Lewis Hayden of the Prince Hall Grand Lodge of Massachusetts, who had escaped slavery himself and hid many fugitives in his house, placed two kegs of explosives in his cellar and announced he would blow up his house, rather than let slave catchers enter. (7)

While in Kentucky, Reverend Bird Parker, pastor of Quinn Chapel A.M.E. Church, Jessie Merriweather, and others, met to organize a Prince Hall Lodge in Louisville. Because of the climate made possible by the Fugitive Slave Act, the members decided to establish their Lodge across the river in New Albany, Indiana, for safety's sake, crossing the Ohio River in skiffs at midnight, sometimes amid high waters and heavy drifts, at the risk of their lives, and then walking five miles to the city to attend Lodge. (8)

Bro. Delany responded to this atrocious law in a speech at Alleghany City, Pennsylvania, in which he proclaimed:

"Honorable Mayor, whatever ideas of liberty I may have, have been received from reading the lives of your revolutionary fathers. I have therein learned that a man has a right to defend his castle with his life, even unto taking of life. Sir, my house is my castle; in that castle are none but my wife and my children, as free as the angels of heaven, and whose liberty is as sacred as the pillars of God. If any man approaches that house in search of a slave, I care not who he may be, whether constable or sheriff, magistrate or even judge of the Supreme Court—nay, let it be he who sanctioned this act to become a law, surrounded by his cabinet as his body guard, with the Declaration of Independence waving above his head as his banner, and the constitution of his country upon his breast as his shield,—if he crosses the threshold of my door, and I do not lay him a lifeless corpse at my feet, I hope the grave may refuse my body a resting place, and righteous Heaven my spirit a home. O, No! He cannot enter that house and we both live." (9)

Of the Masonic life of Bro. Delany there are only brief glimpses recorded in all too brief snatches in printed Masonic historical books, pamphlets, papers and proceedings of various Prince Hall Grand Ldoges. What is known is that Delany found the Masonic bond a "source of strength and comradeship" and an added link tying him to his co-workers fighting for black freedom. Whether he was in Pittsburgh or Canada he found the Masonic fraternity a place of warmth and community with other blacks. (10)

Of his early Masonic beginnings we are indebted for information to his son, also a Prince Hall Mason, Alexander Dumas Delany, who reprinted his father's famous Treatise in 1904, (11) and recorded in the biographical sketch that "early in mature life he joined the Masonic fraternity, taking thirty degrees in his home Lodge in Pittsburgh, and the three side degrees in London, England" (12) a few years subsequent to the publication of the Treatise, which his son writes, "shows the recognition of our order in foreign lands."

A Masonic acquaintance from Scotland explained to this writer, who was attempting to learn if the degrees were received in Scotland, that the expression used by his son, "three side degrees" was in itself interesting. The expression "side degrees" is still current in Scotland for the appendant degrees in the Royal Arch series. These are the degrees of the Royal Arch Mariner, Cryptic Council, Knights of the East and West. A search of the registers of the five Royal Arch Chapters in Glasgow around 1860 found no traces of Bro. Delany's name. There was however at that time an organization called the Early Grand Encampment of Scotland, which controlled all manner of degrees from Templar to Royal Arch. It was of Irish origin. It is possible that Bro. Delany joined Cambuslang No. 5, but records of admission no longer exist as far back as 1860. (13)

Masonically, Bro. Martin R. Delany is better known for his Treatise, *Origin and Objects of Ancient Freemasonry: Its Introduction into the United States, and Legitimacy Among Colored Men*, which he delivered before St. Cyprian Lodge No. 13, June 24th, 1853 in Pittsburgh, and which is the earliest printed work on Prince Hall Freemasonry.

It is here that the Black nationalistic philosophy of Martin R. Delany is best seen. He writes that the Ethiopians are the leading race of mankind, with the Egyptians as a branch of that race, and further suggests the Black origin of Freemasonry:

"In the earliest period of the Egyptian and Ethiopian dynasties, the institution of Masonry was first established. Discovering a defect in the government of man, first suggested an inquiry into his true state and condition. Being a people of a high order of intellect, and subject to erudite and profound thought, the Egyptians and Ethiopians were the first who came to the conclusion that man was created in the similitude of God. This, it will be remembered, was anterior to the Bible record, because Moses was the recorder of the Bible, subsequent to his exodus from Egypt, all his wisdom and ability have been acquired there; as a proof of which, the greatest recommendation to his fitness for so high and holy an office, and the best encomium which that book can possibly bestow upon him in testimony of his qualifications as its scriptor, the Bible itself tells us that Moses was learned in all the wisdom of the Egyptians.

"The Ethiopians early adduced the doctrine and believed in a trinity of the Godhead.

"...While the Africans, who were the authors of this mysterious and beautiful Order, did much to bring it to perfection by the establishment of the great principles of man's likeness to Jehovah in a tribune existence, yet, until the time of King Solomon, there was a great deficiency in his government, in consequence of the policy being monopolized by the priesthood and certain privileged classes of families. For the purpose of remedying what was now conceived to be a great evil in the policy of the world, and for their better government to place wisdom without the acquirement of all men, King Solomon summoned together the united wisdom of the world, men of all nations and races to consider the great project of reducing the mystic ties to a more practical and systematic principle, and stereotyping it with the physical science, by rearing the stupendous and magnificent temple at Jerusalem. For the accomplishment of this masterpiece of all human projects, there were laborers or attendants, mechanics or workmen, and overseers or master-builders. Added to these, there was a designer or originator of all the schemes, an architect or draughtsman, and a furnisher of all the materials for the building, all and every thing of which was classified and arranged after the order of trinity, the building itself, when finished, being composed of an outer, an inner, and a central court.

"After the completion of this great work, the implements of labor having been laid aside, there were scattered to utmost parts of the earth, seventy thousand laborers, eighty thousand workmen, and three thousand and three hundred master builders, making one hundred and fifty-three thousand and three hundred artizans, each of whom having been instructed in all the mysteries of the temple, was fully competent to teach all the arts and sciences acquired at Jerusalem in as many different cities, provinces, states or tribes. At this period, the mysteries assumed the name of Masonry, induced from the building of the temple, and at this time, also commenced the universality of the Order, arising from the going forth of the builders into all parts of the world. This then, was the establishment of Masonry, which has been handed down through all succeeding ages.

"...In many parts of the world, the people of various nations were subject to lose their liberty in several ways. A forfeiture by crime, as in our country; by voluntary servitude for a stipulated sum or reward, as among the Hindoos; and capture in battle and being sold into slavery, as in Algiers. Against these Masonry found it necessary to provide, and accordingly the first two classes were positively proscribed as utterly unworthy of its benefits, as they were equally unworthy of the respectful consideration of the good among mankind. In this, however, was never contemplated the third class of bondees; for none but him who voluntarily comprised his liberty was recognized as a slave by Masons. As there must be a criminal intention in the commission of a crime, so must the act of the criminal be voluntary; hence the criminal and the voluntary bondsmen have both forfeited their Masonic rights by willing degradation. In the case of the captive, an entirely different person is presented before us, who has greater claims upon our sympathies than the untrammeled freeman. Instead of the degraded vassal and voluntary slave, whose prostrate position only facilitates the aspect of his horrible deformity, you have the bold, the brave, the high-minded, the independent-spirit, and manly form of a kindred brother in humanity, whose heart is burning, whose breast is heaving, and whose soul is wrung with panting aspirations for liberty—a commander, a chieftain, a knight, or a prince, it may be—still he is a captive and by the laws of captivity, a slave. Does Masonry, then, contemplate the withholding of its privileges from such applicants as these? Certainly not; since Moses (to whom our great Grand Master Solomon, the founder of the temple, is indebted for his Masonic wisdom) was born and lived in captivity eighty years, and by the laws of his captors a slave. It matters not whether captured in actual conflict, sleeping by the wayside, or in a cradle of bulrushes, after birth, so that there be a longing aspiration for liberty, and manly determination to be free. Policy alone will not permit of the order to confer Masonic privileges on one while yet in captivity; but the fact of his former conditions as such, or that of his parents, can have no bearing whatever on him. The mind and the desires of the recipient must be free; and at the time of his endowment with these privileges, his person and mind must be unencumbered with all earthly trammels or fetters. This is what is meant by Free and Accepted Masonry, to distinguish it from the order when formerly conferred upon the few, like the order of nobility, taking precedence by rank and birth, whether the inheritor was worthy or not of so high and precious privileges.

"...Moses, as before mentioned, of whom the highest encomium is given, is said to have been learned in all the wisdom of the Egyptians, and was not only the descendant of those who had been slaves, but of slave parents, and himself, at the time that he was so taught and instructed in this WISDOM, was a slave! Will it be denied that the man who appeared before the Pharaoh, and was able to perform mystically all that the wisest among the wise men of that mysteriously wise nation was capable of doing, was a Mason? Was not the man who became the Prime Minister and High Priest of Ceremonies among the wise men of Africa, a Mason? If so, will it be disputed that he was legitimately such? Are not we as Masons, and the world of mankind, to him the Egyptian slave—may I not add the fugitive salve—indebted for a transmission to us of the Masonic Records—the Holy Bible, the Word of God? What says the honorable Jacob Brinkerhoof to this? Let a silent tongue answer the inquiry, and listening ear give sanction to his condemnation.

"But if this doctrine held good, according to the acceptation of the term slave, any one who has been deprived of his liberty and thereby rendered politically and socially impotent is a slave; and consequently, Louis Kossuth, ex-Governor of Hungary, bound by the chains of Austria, in the city of Pateya, was, to all intents and purposes, according to this definition, a slave. And when he effected his escape to the United States, was (like Moses from Egypt) a fugitive slave from his masters in Austria, and therefore, by the decrees of the honorable ex-member of Congress, incapable of ever becoming a Mason.

"But Governor Kossuth was made a Mason in Cincinnati, Ohio (14), the resident State of Mr. Brinkerhoof, and therefore, according to him, the Governor is not a Mason at all. He has been a slave!

"...But was the requisition that man should be free born, or free at the time of making them Masons, intended, morally and logically, to apply to those who lost their liberty by any force of invasion and unjust superior power?

"No such thing. In the days of King Solomon, as mentioned elsewhere, there were two classes of men denied masonic privileges: he who lost his liberty by crime, and he, who like Esau, sold his birthright for a mess of pottage—a class bartered away their liberty for a term of years, in consideration of a trifling pecuniary gain. These persons were the same in condition as the Coolies (so called) in China, and the Peons in Mexico, both of whom voluntarily surrendered their rights, at discretion, to another. These persons, and these alone, were provided against, in the wise regulations concerning freedmen, as Masons.

"Did they apply to any others, the patriot, sage, warrior, chieftain, and hero—indeed, the only true brave and chivalric, the most worthy and best specimens of mankind, would be denied a privilege, of which, it would seem, they would be the most legitimate heirs.

"The North American Indians, too, have been enslaved; and yet there has not, to my knowledge, been a syllable spoken or written against their legitimacy; and they, too, are Masons, or have Masonry among them, the facts of which are frequently referred to by white Masonic orators, with pleasureable approbation and pride.

"But to deny to black men the privileges of Masonry, is to deny to a child the lineage of its own parentage. From whence sprung Masonry but from Ethiopia, Egypt, and Assyria, all settled and peopled by the children of Ham?" (15)

The well known Masonic scholar, Silas H. Shepherd in his "Notes on the Literature dealing with Prince Hall Masonry," wrote of Delany's work that "The first part of his treatise shows that he followed the traditions of such writers as Anderson, Preston, and Oliver, in addition to bringing in traditions of Africa, with which he has something in common with Albert Churchward's *Signs and Symbols of Primordial Man*, in that he credits Africa with being the place where Freemasonry originated. The main feature of the treatise is, however, to show the legitimate origin of Freemasonry among colored men and the subject is handled with skill and ability. Robert F. Gould warns against reading books that are inclined to stress tradition and treat the traditions as history; but if we can read theories that are far short of historical accuracy to get former conceptions with some degree of satisfaction, it should not be dangerous to read the theories of this talented colored Mason on Moses deriving his wisdom from the Ethiopians. The Mason who has the opportunity to read this treatise will find keen enjoyment and many profitable suggestions, for it is written in true Masonic spirit." (16)

Another brief reference is provided by Charles H. Wesley's *History of the Prince Hall Grand Lodge of Ohio* that Bro. Delany, then Master of St. Cyprian Lodge in 1847, played a significant role in initiating seven Masons from Cincinnati, who later were chartered as Corinthian Lodge No. 17 by the Grand Lodge of Pennsylvania, which became the cornerstone of the "Mother of Masonic Lodges" the Prince Hall Grand Lodge of Ohio, as Corinthian Lodge No. 1. (17)

It is also known that Bro. Delany was appointed District Deputy of the Western District at the organization of the National Grand Lodge or National Compact in 1847. (18)

Little else is known of Bro. Delany's active participation in Masonry, other than the fact that twenty seven years later at the Semi-Annual Communication of the Prince Hall Grand Lodge of Pennsylvania, June 24, 1874, its sadly recorded that "The Committee on Appeals reported that in the case of Bro. Martin R. Delany that he had inquired and received a letter from St. Cyprian Lodge No. 13, stating that he had been suspended for non-payment of dues some 14 years back. That he had been written to with no response on his part.

"Further, that before leaving Pittsburgh, over fifteen years since, he borrowed $50.00 from the Lodge, which he never repaid:

"That, not withstanding, had the Brother applied for reinstatement, they, no doubt, would have done so.

"The Committee therefore report that from the evidence of the records he is a suspended member.

"Resolved, that the Report of the Committee be approved.

"Moved that the appeal of M. R. Delany be returned to him with our disapproval. Moved that the statement just read from the W. Master of St. Cyprian Lodge No. 13 be forwarded to the M. W. National Grand Master, with the request that it may be read in the Grand Lodge of South Carolina. Carried!" (19)

This writer is not certain that this was the end of his brilliant active Masonic life; further inquiry would have to be made, but of Bro. Delany it must be said that he served Prince Hall Freemasonry, the Craft and his people well.

Major Martin R. Delany, U.S.A. Past Master, Past District Deputy Grand Master

ORIGIN AND OBJECTS

OF

ANCIENT FREEMASONRY;

ITS

INTRODUCTION INTO THE UNITED STATES,

AND

LEGITIMACY AMONG COLORED MEN.

A TREATISE DELIVERED BEFORE

St. Cyprian Lodge, No 13, June 24th, A. D. 1853----A. L. 5853.

BY

M. R. DELANY, K. M., D. D. G. H. P.

"Great is Truth, and must prevail

PITTSBURGH:

PRINTED BY W S HAVEN, CORNER MARKET AND SECOND STREETS

1853.

Title Page of earliest printed work on Negro Freemasonry

REFERENCES FOR PART VIII

1. Peter M. Bergman, *The Chronological History of the Negro in America*, New York, Evanston and London, Harper & Row Publishers, 1969, p. 97.

2. Frank A. Rollins, *Life and Public Services of Martin R. Delany [New York, Arno Press and the New York Times, 1969], p. ii*

3. William Loren Katz, *Eyewitness: The Negro in American History*, New York, Toronto, London, Pitman Publishing Corporation, 1967, p. 142-143.

4. Martin R. Delany and Robert Campbell, *Search for a Place, Black Separatism and Africa, 1860.* The University of Michigan—Ann Arbor Paper-back, 1971. It is interesting to note that while in the Republic of Liberia Bro. Delany was in the company of Past President Joseph J. Roberts and Charles B. Dunbar, who would both serve as Grand Master of this African Prince Hall Grand Lodge. President Roberts served three years and Dunbar, two.

5. Rollins, *op. cit.*, p. 171.

6. *Ibid*, p. 29.

7. Katz, *op. cit.*, p. 189.

8. *Prince Hall Masonic Yearbook, 1968*, Published under the auspieces of the Grand Master's Conference of Prince Hall Masons of America, p. 91.

9. Rollins, *op. cit*, p. 76.

10. *Martin R. Delany, The Beginnings of Black Nationalism*, by Victor Ullman, p. 193, cited by William Alan Muraskin, *Middle-Class Blacks in a White Society—Prince Hall Freemasonry in America*, Berkeley, Los Angeles, London, University of California Press, 1975, p. 53.

11. Martin R. Delany, *Origin and Objects of Ancient Freemasonry; Its Introduction into the United States and Legitimacy among Colored Men—*A Treatise delivered before St. Cyprian Lodge No. 13, June 24th A.D. 1853 A.L. 5853, Pittsburgh, W. S. Haven, Corner Market and Second Street, 1853. Re-published by A. D. Delany, Xenia, Ohio, 1904.

12. While in England, Bro. Delany was associated with Henry Peter Brougham (Lord Brougham and Vaux called by Delany, the unflinching friend of the Negro) (1778-1868), Lord High Chancellor of England from 1830. B. Sept. 19, 1778 at Edinburgh, Scotland. With Sydney Smith and Jeffrey, founded the *Edinburgh Review* in 1802. Practiced at the English bar in 1808 and member of parliament in 1810. He carried the measure making slave trade a felony and defended Queen Caroline as her attorney general in trial (1820). He was a founder of London Univ. in 1828 and by a famous speech in 1831 helped pass the Reform Bill. He was the original "learned friend" in Peacock's *Crochet Castle*. The brougham (carriage) is named after him. He was initiated, passed and raised in Fortrose Lodge, Stornoway, Scotland on Aug. 20, 21, 1799 and on June 24, 1800 affiliated with

Canongate Kilwinning Lodge in Edinburgh. D. May 7, 1868; see William R. Denslow, *10,000 Famous Freemasons* (Missouri Lodge of Research, 1957.) p. 136.

13. It was thought by this writer that Bro. Delany may have received his "three side degrees" while attending the Congress of the National Association for the Promotion of Social Science at Glasgow, Scotland, in September 1860, but a letter from George Draffen of Newington, MBE, OSTJ, The Supreme Council for Scotland of the thirty-third and last degree of the Ancient and Accepted Scottish Rite to this writer does not bear this out.

14. Lajos (Louis) Kossuth (1802-1894) Hungarian patriot and statesman. b. in 1802 at Monok, Hungary. Imprisoned by Austrian government on political charges from 1837-40, during which time he taught himself English. In 1841, he became editor of the *Pesti Hirlap*, prominent Hungarian daily newspaper, and through its pages presented his liberal views. The liberal party seated him as finance minister in the government of 1848. He persuaded the Hugarian national assembly to declare independence from Austria (1848-49), and he was appointed governor of Hungary with dictatorial powers. When the insurrection was crushed, Aug. 11, 1849, Kossuth fled into exile in Turkey, where he was imprisoned from 1849-51, and finally released by the intervention of the U.S., which sent the *U.S. Mississippi* to bring him to London; later he came to the U.S., residing in this country in 1851-52. He then returned to England and remained there serveral years. In 1859 he went to Italy, where he organized an Hungarian Legion and rendered valiant service to the Italian liberators, Mazzini and Garibaldi, qq.v. He lived in Italy the rest of his life, dying at Turin, March 20, 1894, at the age of 91. On Feb. 18, 1852, Cincinnati Lodge No. 133, Cincinnati, Ohio, received an extraordinary letter. It was a hand written petition from Kossuth: "To the Worshipful Master, Wardens and Brethren of Cincinnati Lodge No. 133 of Free and Accepted Masons. The petition of the subscriber respectfully showeth that having long entertained a favorable opinion of your ancient institution, he is desirous of being admitted a member thereof if found worthy. Being an exile for liberty's sake, he has now no fixed place of residence, is now staying at Cincinnati; his age is 49 1/2 years, his occupation is to restore his native land, Hungary, to its national independence, and to achieve by community of action with other nations, civil and religious liberty in Europe. Louis Kossuth." At the same time petitions were received from the following members of his staff—Col. Count Gregory Bethlen, Peter A. Nagi, Paul Hajnik, and Ulius Utosy Strasser. The petitions were made a case of emergency, and the next day they were initiated (Feb. 19) and passed, and raised the following day. Kossuth and his staff also became members of Cincinnati Chapter No. 2 R.A.M., according to Dr. James J. Tyler, historian of the Grand Lodge of Ohio. On Feb. 28, 1852, Kossuth attended a meeting of Center Lodge No. 23, Indianapolis, and ad-

dressed the Lodge, followed by a visit to St. Johns Lodge No. 1 of Newark, N.J. On May 10, 1852 he addressed the Grand Lodge of Massachusetts, see William R. Denslow, *op. cit.*, p. 39-40.

15. Martin R. Delany, *Origin and Objects*, etc., *op. cit.*, published in the *Phylaxis Magazine*, July, September and December 1976 issues. (Phylaxis Society, Volume II, Number 6, 7 and 8.)

16. Silas H. Shepherd, *An Invaluable Bibliography*. The National Trestle Board, March 1922, p. 29. Brother Shepherd was Chairman of Masonic Research of the Caucasian Grand Lodge of Wisconsin.

17. Charles H. Wesley, *The History of the Prince Hall Grand Lodge of the State of Ohio, 1849-1960*, Wilberforce, Ohio, Central State College Press, 1961, p. 57. In a letter dated July 18, 1963, written by Harold V. B. Voorhis, author of *Negro Masonry in the United States* (1940), then an advocate of the regularity of Prince Hall Masonry, having twenty-three years later made a complete about face, Voorhis addressed to Brother Jerry Marsengill of the Caucasian Grand Lodge of Iowa, author of *Negro Masonry in Iowa*, who at the time was collecting data for his book wrote "...if you are going to try and show the derivation of the Ohio Grand Lodge...you have a problem!" This rather pointed observation by Voorhis is in conflict with the official history as written by Bro. Wesley. Voorhis, Masonic researcher, historian and writer, in his attempt to discredit Prince Hall Masonry, made the same mistakes most Caucasian Masonic historians make in researching the Black experience, and not having any personal experience with the Black community, cannot understand that Blacks, for the most part, did not leave the kind of records which allow a traditional historical approach to research. This is not to necessarily condemn the writings of all Caucasians who have attempted to scientifically inquire into the Masonic history of the Black man, but for the large part most can be dismissed, because of their lack of full understanding of the race. Their research cannot be complete without exploring the full range of the Black experience and then understanding it. A good example of this is William Alan Muraskin's *Middle-Class Blacks in a White Society: Prince Hall Freemasonry in America*. Mr. Muraskin's knowledge of Black written history, Masonic and otherwise, is great, but his knowledge of the race is limited, and many of the points raised in his book show that Prince Hall Freemasons still "jive" Caucasians.

18. Harry E. Davis, *A History of Freemasonry Among Negroes in America*, United Supreme Council, A.A.S.R., Northern Jurisdiction, U.S.A. Prince Hall Affiliation, Inc., 1946, p. 272.

19. *Proceedings of the Most Worshipful Prince Hall Grand Lodge F. & A.M. of Pennsylvania*, 1874, p. 96.

IX

PART 1

THE MASONIC PHILOSOPHY OF SAMUEL W. CLARK

One of the saddest things about controversy is that it frequently obscures every other element concerning a topic except the point controverted. Colored Masonry has suffered much from this blight of controversy. In Masonic, as well as in political history, the Negro has been the vortex around which a veritable torrent of passion has whirled. In the midst of these tempests men do not take time to assemble and analyze simple facts, the scientific pose is lost, the historian is superseded by the advocate, and a wealth of information is neglected." (1) Throughout the history of the Black man in America, Masonic as well as political, have appeared on the stage, some of the most eloquent spokesmen this country has ever produced. They were not only eloquent, but dedicated Prince Hall Freemasons, whose only weapons were words and the justness of their cause. Words placed on paper so many years ago are yet still alive—passionate words to combat the prejudice and racism of the past, as well as the present. Their names are held in reverence and deep respect by Masonic scholars around the world: Prince Hall, Lewis Hayden, Martin R. Delany, John T. Hilton, Harry A. Williamson, Arthur A. Schomburg, Harry E. Davis and scores of others.

No voice was more eloquent or more forceful than the Masonic writings and philosophy of Samuel Wilcox Clark. Of him was truthfully said "his was a voice of one crying in the wilderness during the dark days of our Masonic history." (2)

His work *Negro Mason in Equity* and his memorable words are worthy to be remembered throughout the Prince Hall fraternity. Bro. Clark was born in Cincinnati, Ohio, July 25, 1846. He was initiated and raised in 1870 in True American Lodge No. 2, in Cincinnati and served that Prince Hall Jurisdiction as Grand Master from 1879 to 1888, and again from 1898 to 1902. (3)

In 1886 the then Grand Master Clark published in the Proceedings of the Grand Lodge his *Negro Mason in Equity*, which was later published as a pamphlet. Grand Master Barnes of Michigan praised Clark and this work by saying, "few jurisdictions have produced his equal in Masonic knowledge and untiring devotion to the fraternity. His name will live as long as Masonry exists among Colored Men." (4)

His legacy can be found in his philosophy, and his attacks upon the White Masonic power structure of his day. His appeal was for truth and justice before the world Masonic community, and against hypocrisy.

"The time is full at hand when we must no longer depend upon our friends to do battle for us. The fight must be our own. Neither must it be a defensive one, we must be aggressive, we must assert ourselves, we must tear away the flimsy mask behind which the White American Mason takes refuge from the penetrating eye of truth and justice. Let us turn upon him the fierce light of recorded history, thereby disclosing to the open gaze of the world the false, unjust, and un-Masonic position which he assumes." (5)

His appeals stand as meaningful today, as when they were first penned.

"Masons of the world, wheresoever dispersed, the Negro Mason of America stands before you today as a just and upright Mason, and as such demands that you shall try him by the Square of Virtue, and having tried him and found him just and true, he further demands that you deny him not, but that you receive him and accept him, accord unto him all of the rights that may belong to him. He does not make this demand because he is a Negro, neither does he ask that you do this as a favor, but he demands it because he is a Mason as you are, and because his right to the title of Free and Accepted Mason is equal to yours—no more, no less!" (6)

Although American Masonry praised Albert Pike, who was one of the most distinguished Masons America has produced, the negrophobic Confederate General was author of *Morals and Dogma*, often classed as the most profound Masonic work written in the United States. His public utterance justifies it being judged as the writings of a hypocritical, prejudiced, racist Mason. His famous statement that he would renounce Masonry rather than recognize Negro Masons as brothers (7), and his further assertion that by the Convention of Lausanne, the Scottish Rite was saved from contamination by the "leprosy of Negro association" (8) led Clark to ask:

"What think you of a man professing to be a Mason uttering such sentiments as these... God pity Brother Pike and the thousands of canting hypocrites like him." (9)

"While, we know there are large numbers of White Masons who acknowledge the justness of our claims, and stand ready and willing to try us and not deny us, we also feel and know that there is a vaster and a mightier number who, knowing all these things to be true, yet reject us and deny us. You ask what motive can impel these men—Men whose eloquent utterance, in chaste and beautiful language, have bid the world to pause and gaze upon the matchless symmetry of our grand and noble institution, and contemplate in awe the grandeur and sublimity of its principles—to reject the truth? It is that slimy coated and cold-blooded serpent of prejudice against the Negro. You see it in every feeble and tottering imbecile and in the little prattling child, wherever you turn the monster, with his ever-open, glassy eye, is staring at you. No place is secure from his intrusion; go to the halls of justice and you will find him there, and even within the sacred portals of God's tabernacles does he stealthily crawl, not even sparing the altar where the humble Christian kneels to take the consecrated emblems of our Lord and Saviour. This is why we are denied, this is why we are rejected, this is why we are termed 'clandestine, illegal and irregular.' " (10)

Two reasons, states Clark, may be given for this unjust position taken by the White Masons of the United States, first:

"The general ignorance of the great mass of American Masons concerning our (Prince Hall) origin and history, the bitter prejudice, which seems many Americans have against the Negro. This prejudice, which seems to be almost inherent, if not wholly so, renders them unfit to do justice to the Negro Mason..." (11)

And of the false claims of Caucasian Masonic historians, Clark wrote:

"The White Masonic historians, knowing of the many irregularities of their early organization, seek many ways to find excuses and make apologies for them!" (12)

And of the greatest offender of them all, Clark scoffs:

"What a commentary here upon the attitude of the Grand Lodge of Massachusetts towards the Negro Masons of America, who can show by the very records brought to light by her, a clearer and better title to legitimacy than either Massachusetts or New Hampshire. Does it need a seer to tell the reason of this unjust discrimination? Shame! Shame! Shame!!!" (13)

"They either refuse to examine the records of history for fear they may discover that the Negro's right is equal to theirs, or, knowing the facts, endeavor to subvert them by misstatements and false reasoning!" (14)

Above all, Clark remained a realist.

"But we say to him [the Caucasian historian] your professions are not sustained by [your] works, and that you do give the lie to your words, when you say you believe in the Brotherhood of Man!" (15)

Clark was above all a proud Mason, who declared:

"As Negro Masons, we need expect no recognition from organized White American Masons. I plead for none; I care for none at the sacrifice of honor and dignity. I stand as just, as true, as pure a Free Mason as ever trod God's green earth. My title is as perfect as that of the Prince of Wales, or the President of the United States, as he who travels with the caravan over the desert or he who dwells on the plains of the far west. Wherever he may be upon the continents of the land or the islands of the sea, if he be a Free Mason he is my brother and cannot deny me if he would!" (16)

Upon the death of this scholarly Prince Hall Mason the following resolution was submitted at the 1903 Grand Lodge Session of the Prince Hall Grand Lodge of Ohio by Joseph L. Jones and adopted:

WHEREAS: This M. W. Grand Lodge having authorized the publication of the second edition of "The Negro Mason in Equity," written by our lamented M. W. Past Grand Master, Samuel W. Clark,

BE IT RESOLVED: That we recommend that there be added to this work the funeral oration as delivered by R. W. Bro. Alexander Morris, Grand Orator, the two being combined, printed and sold for the purpose of placing a Masonic monument upon the grave of our distinguished brother, as a mark of the esteem in which he was held by the Craft.

In concluding an address to the Prince Hall Grand Lodge of Ohio, Grand Master Clark had declined a further re-election and had used these words:

"There is a very beautiful story told in one of the books of an eminent author, in which he describes an angel as coming down from heaven to see what men live by. After a sojourn of more than two years upon the earth and an association with all grades of society, the angel discovered that men live by love. They may have wealth, station, reputation, and renown, but unless their lives and their communion with their fellow men be crowned with love, they live in vain." (17)

What better way to end this portion of the chapter. This writer believes that the greatest monument befitting the memory of Bro. Clark would be the mandatory reading of his classic, *The Negro*

Samuel W. Clark, Twelfth Grand Master, 1879-1888

Mason in Equity, by each and every Prince Hall Freemason. Not to glorify this splendid work, as it can stand on its own merit, but to educate the mass of the fraternity to their history, and to *"Render unto Caesar the things which are Caesar's."*

PART 2

THE STORM THAT PRODUCED LIGHT
ON A DARK SUBJECT

By the beginning of the twentieth century, the Caucasian Grand Lodge of Washington stretched forth a hand of friendship to Prince Hall Freemasonry and found itself swirling in a sea of passion, controversy and hostility the like of which had never before been witnessed in American Freemasonry.

In 1897, two Prince Hall Masons, Bros. Gideon S. Bailey and Con A. Rideout, both residing in the State of Washington, petitioned the Caucasian Grand Lodge of that State to "devise some way" whereby they might be "brought into communication" with members of the Craft in the State.

The petition was referred to a committee of three: Thomas M. Reed, James E. Edmiston and William H. Upton, two being Past Grand Masters. (1) The committee made a year long exhaustive study and submitted its report to the Grand Lodge at its communication in 1898, and the report was approved by a practically unanimous vote. (2) The Committee recommended for adoption:

1. Asserted the right of its subordinates to recognize all Negroes made in Lodges descended from Prince Hall.

2. Declared African Grand Lodge, and the two Black Grand Lodges in Pennsylvania, legitimate Grand bodies.

3. Stated Prince Hall Lodges and Grand Lodges established in the State of Washington would not be deemed an invasion of its jurisdiction.

4. Extended its sympathy to Prince Hall Masons.

5. Declared that race or color is not a proper test to apply to a candidate. (3)

Between October 1898 and June 1899, sixteen Caucasian Grand Lodges declared "non-intercourse" with this Grand Lodge and some even dared attack its very sovereignty.

The Caucasian Grand Lodge of Florida, meeting at its 70th Annual Communication, brazenly declared that the Grand Lodge of Washington was "invading on (sic) its rights and territory." (4)

At the 82nd Annual Communication of the Caucasian Grand Lodge of Indiana, held in Indianapolis, May 23, 1899, the Grand Master appointed a special committee, which reported that the Grand Lodge of Washington was ill advised and that its actions were uncalled for and resolved in very forceful language to sever fraternal relations with said Grand Lodge. (5)

On June 6, 1899, the Grand Lodge of Iowa, in its 56th Annual Communication in Mason City, a city originally known as "Shibboleth" and later as "Masonic Grove," a city founded by a number of Freemasons, (6) likewise formed a special committee which reported in part:

> "Sincerely regretting the action of Washington in renewing the agitation, and regarded such action as ill advised and well calculated to disturb the harmony of the fraternity." (7)

The Caucasian Grand Lodge of Alabama, meeting in Montgomery in its 78th Annual Communication, December 6, 1898, stated that "Masonry being pre-eminently social, the social equality of the Whites and Blacks is imperiously asserted by the former." (8)

Arizona, at its 17th Annual Communication, held in Globe, November 15, 1898, called the actions of Washington "unwarranted because it transgresses an unwritten law."

But none reached the baseness of the Caucasian Grand Lodge of Kentucky, meeting in its 99th Annual Session in Louisville, October 18, 1898, when it declared the action to be "undignified and unmasonic, revolutionary and uncalled for!" This conservative remark was made by Grand Master H. R. Thompson. (9) The matter was brought before a special committee for final action. The report was read by the Grand Secretary who disgracefully stated that "Your committee shall, as have other Masonic writers, refrain from commenting upon any remarks made by Grand Master Thompson, for the reason that since they were made, he has in all probability joined Prince Hall, in the Grand Lodge above, where it is to be presumed that even Kentuckians associate with Negroes." (10)

In the words of Samuel W. Clark, "What think you of a man professing to be a Mason uttering such sentiments as these...?"

In Louisiana, at its 78th Annual Communication, held in New Orleans, February 13, 1899, the subject was given little attention and referred to a special committee as a matter of form, as the Constitution of this Grand Lodge reads, "A candidate for the degrees of Freemasonry must be a White man!" (11)

As the printed proceedings from Washington's sister Grand Lodges became available, it became evident that they presumed to sit in judgment without any adequate study of the question. In most cases they showed a complete ignorance of Masonic law and Prince Hall Masonic history.

Because of these un-Masonic attacks and criticism heaped upon it, the Grand Lodge of Washington felt compelled to justify itself in the eyes of the reasonable Masons at home and abroad. It printed in pamphlet form the report of its Committee on Correspondence under the title *Light on a Dark Subject*. This pamphlet evolved into the book *Negro Masonry being a Critical Examination* by William H. Upton.

While the bitter attacks were being leveled at Washington, the M. W. Prince Hall Grand Lodge of Massachusetts, meeting in Boston, December 21, 1899, took note of the growing storm, and Grand Master Fred M. Douglass wrote:

"There was nothing in the character of the resolutions of the Grand Lodge of Washington to warrant the abuse and denunciation which followed. They were cautious and conservative, with greater negative than positive strength, and however liberally the spirit of them might have been interpreted, that spirit would have been denied expression outside of the State of Washington. But a hue and cry was raised and under the dominating strength of bitter, unreasoning prejudice, by the time the Annual Communication of 1899, more than a score of professedly Masonic American Grand Lodges had declared non-intercourse, and six others...had threatened it unless the action was repealed.

"At the Annual Communication of 1899, the controversy was referred to a committee of seven Past Grand Masters as follows.... The report which was accepted with but two dissenting votes, reaffirms the first resolution and in pointed words calls attention to the un-Masonic character of those Grand Lodges which by direct legislation have excluded men because of the color of their skin; repeals the second resolution and then adds that their relations with the United Grand Lodge of England have been and are of such a fraternal nature they can not with courtesy to that Grand Lodge refuse to allow their constituency to continue to recognize as legitimate Masons, men initiated in Lodges existing by authority originally derived from the Grand Lodge of England (Modern), the Grand Lodge of England (Ancient), or the United Grand Lodge formed by the union of these two in 1813, so long as the regularity of such initiations continues to be recognized by the United Grand Lodge of England. This simply removes the claim of colored Masons to legitimacy from the American Lodge to the Grand Lodge of England.

"The third resolution was repeated without comment and does not pledge the Grand Lodge to hostile legislation should colored Masons enter the jurisdiction. The situation, so far as colored Masons are concerned, is practically unchanged.

"The direct recognition of colored Masons is rescinded and a report has been adopted in its stead under cover of which colored Masons receive whatever of benefit was conferred by the acts of 1898. The attack of these Grand Lodges upon the Grand Lodge of Washington adds one more to the many blows aimed at the life of the law of exclusive Grand Lodge territorial jurisdiction. Under this law a Grand Lodge is supposed to be supreme and independent of all authority, save the Landmarks and its own constitution, within its jurisdiction. But their action says the legislation of a Grand Lodge within its jurisdiction is to be subjected to the will and pleasure of Grand Lodges without. Our white brethren may not have had a National Grand Lodge at any time in their history, but when they invoke the concerted action of a majority of the American Grand Lodges to coerce the Grand Lodge of Washington, they certainly employed National Grand Lodge powers!" (12)

When knowledge of the declaration by the Washington Committee of three reached the Caucasian Grand Lodge of Massachusetts, it was among the most disturbed. However, a report made forty-nine years later (1947) by a similar committee appointed to investigate the subject of Prince Hall Freemasonry in Massachusetts coincided with the Washington report adopted in 1898, to such an extent that the average Masonic student may well consider them in agreement. (13)

The depth and intensity of P.G.M. Upton's feelings are exemplified by a provision in his will that no monument be erected over his grave until both white and black Masons could stand beside it as brothers. The day has yet to come!

Bro. Upton generously turned over the rights to the publication of his famous *Negro Masonry* to the Most Worshipful Prince Hall Grand Lodge of Massachusetts.

In an article appearing in the August-September 1917 issue of *The American Freemason* under title of *The Position and Plea of Negro Masonry,*" by Harry A. Williamson, noted that:

"The late Brother William H. Upton, Grand Master of Washington whose name is and will forever be inseparable from this subject, is remembered with a growing respect by his white, and with admiration and gratitude by his colored brethren. The editor of *The American Freemason* is not alone in the expressed opinion that Brother Upton was far and away the most scholarly Mason the United States has yet produced. His judicial mind peculiarly fitted him to determine and analyze the evidence as to the legitimacy of colored Masonry, and his judgments have proven unassailable. The mean flings and sneers that greeted him were but exhibitions of men of lesser mind, who would not frame answers to his agruments.

"Brother Upton found that in his time the scholars of the Craft were able to divest themselves of prejudice, and were even then at one in acknowledging the legitimacy of the Lodges deriving from African Lodge No. 459.... . The bitter controversy that followed upon Upton's report, and upon the action of the Grand Lodge of Washington, has now died away. The little group of Masonic students and scholars of that time, has since grown to be a large and influential element in American Masonry. It is unlikely that a present successor to Brother Upton would have to meet such storm of abuse and unreasoning opposition in any attempt to point out the way of justice and true fraternity. Yet, unfortunately it still holds true, so far as white officialdom is concerned, and as was expressed by the Past Grand Master of Washington, that 'men whose utterances fail to disclose ever a superficial acquaintance with either the history or the law, have presumed to sit in judgment on this important subject.' "

In summarizing his article, Bro. Williamson exhorted fair-minded Masonic students to read the proceedings of that period and if:

"followed dispassionately, and the frequent appeals to prejudice so openly made therein are ignored, the inquirer will be profoundly impressed by the un-Masonic bitterness displayed by men who could apparently deal only in invective. Also he will observe the calmness and clarity of statement that characterized the writings of Upton and the few who were with him at the time."

The Prince Hall fraternity noted the passing of Bro. Upton within the pages of their respective Grand Lodge proceedings with New York setting aside two pages as a memorial. (14)

On Decoration Day, 1920, at the request of the Prince Hall Grand Lodge of New York, M.W. Ernest H. Holmes, Grand Master of the Prince Hall Grand Lodge of Washington covered Upton's grave with a blanket of flowers. (15) While a movement was suggested by the Prince Hall fraternity to erect a substantial memorial at Upton's grave site, this did not materialize. (16)

In 1921, there appeared briefly William H. Upton Lodge No. 11 at Lewiston, Mont., but it has since disappeared. However, today in Richburg, South Carolina under the jurisdiction of the Prince Hall Grand Lodge of that State, there is active William Upton Lodge No. 145, which is named for this outstanding and exceptional white Freemason. (17)

In 1980, the Phylaxis Society, a Masonic research organization of Prince Hall Freemasons, named Past Grand Master Upton to its Masonic Hall of Fame, and at its Sixth Annual Session, held in Tacoma, Washington, presented the Caucasian Grand Lodge of Washington, an appropriate plaque in honor of Upton. (18)

PART 3

CAUCASIAN PRINCE HALL LODGE

Portions of this were taken from *A Chronological History of Prince Hall Masonry 1788-1932*, by Harry A. Williamson, by permission of the Schomburg Center for Research in Black Culture, The New York Public Library, Astor, Lenox and Tilden Foundations.

One of the most interesting facts in Masonic history is to be found in the minute book of the Most Worshipful Prince Hall Grand Lodge of New York, under the proceedings for the year 1871. Here is to be found a Lodge of German Jews working under the authority of this Prince Hall Grand Lodge.

This Lodge, designated as either "Downshire" or "Progress" No. 12, was located in New York City and warranted February 3, 1870. Its members were all Hebrews of German extraction. The only American born Black member was Brother Albert Wilson, its Secretary, who at the same time was Secretary of the Grand Lodge.

It is recorded that from February to December of 1870, this Lodge held twelve regular communications. The well-known Prince Hall Masonic scholar, Bro. Harry E. Davis, of the Prince Hall Grand Lodge of Ohio, author of *A History of Freemasonry Among Negroes in America*, states that the warrant was recalled, as some of these brethren returned to Europe at the time of the Franco-Prussian War. Bro. Harry A. Williamson in his *A Chronological History of Prince Hall Masonry 1784-1932* adds that the members remaining ultimately transferred their membership to the Caucasian Grand Lodge of that State. In support of this statement, Bro. Williamson records the proceedings of the Prince Hall Grand Lodge for 1874:

"Progress Lodge No. 12, New York City, changed to Shakespeare Lodge No. 750 under the Jurisdiction of the New York Grand Lodge (white)."

Bro. Williamson and Bro. Davis state that in a further record pertaining to the above statement, information was obtained in 1910, through one of the members, a Bro. B. Le Vene, who was then a member of Wm. McKinley Lodge 840, under the jurisidiction of the Caucasian Grand Lodge of New York. He stated that he had been a member of the Prince Hall Lodge and that the first two degrees were re-conferred on him when he transferred his membership to the Caucasian body, but not the third as his raising under the Prince Hall Jurisdiction was deemed sufficient.

Bro. Williamson states that the records of Downshire No. 12, as noted in the minutes of the Prince Hall Grand Lodge reads:

"Downshire Lodge No. 12, organized February 3rd (Thursday), 1870. We are in possession of reports from this Lodge under dates of November 30, 1870, September, October, and December 1871. An appeal addressed to the Grand Lodge September 7, 1870, is signed in the handwriting of the following Brethren:

    M. W. Abraham Levy
    S. W. D. Jones
    J. W. Acting, Julius Cohn."

In the Williamson Prince Hall Masonic collection, housed in the New York Public Library, is a report sheet submitted to the Prince Hall Grand Lodge in 1870, showing the following named members:

1. Abraham Levy	14. Samuel Lener
2. Dramin Jones	15. John Delvert
3. Abram Newfeldt	16. Simon Goldstein
4. Tobias Cohen	17. Solomon Goldstein
5. Herman Holzwasser	18. Morris Goldstein
6. David Cerciwitz	19. Henry Levy
7. Jacob Goldfarb	20. Julius Cohn
8. Henry Rosenthal	21. Sol. Alexander
9. Marcus Rosenthal	22. Moritz Brookman
10. Zundel Hebstein	23. Meyer Rosenthal
11. Morris Isaacs	24. Ossac Wasseioug
12. Max Levy	25. John Brown
13. Abraham Newmark	

Additional facts from the records read as follows:

"Twelve (12) regular communications, three (3) initiations, two (2) crafting—one raised. Rejected one (1)—Mr. Nathan Israel. Reinstated two (2) Bros. Sol. Goldstein and John Cooper. Affiliated one (1) Bro. John Bowles, initiated Bros. Aaron Oppenheim, William Rosenthal, Jacob Levy, Buried one (1) Samuel Laner."

The above statistics are from the report of the Most Worshipful Prince Hall Grand Lodge of New York of September 1, 1871, and are without parallel in the annals of Prince Hall Masonic history. (1)

All three parts of this chapter are interesting aspects of Prince Hall Masonic history. The next Chapter begins a new page in Prince Hall Masonry.

REFERENCES FOR PART 1

1. Harry E. Davis, *A History of Freemasonry Among Negroes in America*, United Supreme Council, A.A.S.R., Northern Jurisdiction, U.S.A., Prince Hall Affiliation, Inc., 1946, p. 5.

2. Address of Grand Master Robert C. Barnes, 39th Annual Communication of the Prince Hall Grand Lodge of Michigan, Battle Creek, Tuesday, January 26, 1904.

3. Charles H. Wesley, *The History of the Prince Hall Grand Lodge of Free and Accepted Masons of the State of Ohio 1849-1960*, Wilberforce, Ohio: Central State College Press, 1969, p. 90, 91.

4. Barnes, *op. cit.*

5. Samuel W. Clark, *The Negro Mason in Equity*, M.W. Prince Hall Grand Lodge of Free and Accepted Masons for the State of Ohio, 1886, p. 3.

6. *Ibid*, p. 68.

7. Views of General Albert Pike, Sovereign Grand Commander, Ancient and Accepted Scottish Rite of Freemasonry, letter to John D. Caldwell, September 13, 1875 cited by John D. Caldwell, *"New Day—New Duty"* Reports, Memorials, etc., to the M.W. Grand Lodge of Ohio (Caucasian), relative to Colored Grand Lodge F. & A.M. of Ohio, Cincinnati, 1875, p. 50 and William H. Upton, *Negro Masonry being a Critical Examination*, Cambridge, 1902, p. 214.

8. Harry E. Davis, 33⁰, *The Scottish Rite in the Prince Hall Fraternity*, The United Supreme Council, A.A.S.R., Prince Hall Affiliation, 1940, p. 28. Davis writes, "And yet in the face of this, when Pike completed his monumental work on the Scottish Rite, he turned over a complete set to Ill. Thornton Jackson, then Sovereign Grand Commander of the Prince Hall Southern Jurisdiction. His gifts are as follows:

    1. Morals and Dogma.
    2. Liturgy of the Ancient and Accepted Scottish Rite 1-3⁰; 4-14⁰; 15-18⁰; 19-30⁰; 31-32⁰.
    3. Grand Constitution of 1762.
    4. Latin Grand Constitution of 1786 and the Statutes of the Supreme Council, Southern Jurisdiction U.S.A., published by authority of the Supreme Council in 1859.
    5. The 33⁰.

These works are in the library of the Prince Hall Southern Jurisdiction. It is hard to reconcile Pike's action and words, but his conduct is clearly one of those curious contradictions so often found in race relations in America. An older generation of Prince Hall Masons assert that Pike had all the prejudices of his slave-holding caste. He was violently opposed to the recognition or absorption of colored Masons. But, they say, he was perfectly willing that the Prince Hall Craft function as an independent fraternity. With this explanation it is possible to partly reconcile the utterances and deeds of this great Masonic scholar.

9. Clark, *op. cit.*,p. 62.

10. *Ibid*, p. 60.

11. *Ibid*, p. 4.

12. *Ibid*, p. 23.

13. *Ibid*, p. 38.

14. *Ibid*, p. 4.

15. *Ibid*, p. 11.

16. Address of Grand Master Samuel W. Clark, 50th Annual Communication of the Prince Hall Grand Lodge of Ohio, 1899.

17. Address of Grand Master Samuel W. Clark, August 22, 1888, M.W. Prince Hall Grand Lodge of Ohio.

REFERENCE FOR PART II

1. William H. Upton, *Negro Masonry Being a Critical Examination*, Cambridge, Mass., The M. W. Prince Hall Grand Lodge of Massachusetts, 1902, Chapter 1.

2. *Ibid*, p. 2.

3. Harry E. Davis, *A History of Freemasonry Among Negroes in America*, United Supreme Council, A.A.S.R., Northern Jurisdiction, U.S.A., P.H.A., Inc., 1946, p. 156, and Proceedings of the Grand Lodge of Washington, 1898, p. 60.

4. The Proceedings of the M. W. Prince Hall Grand Lodge of Missouri, 1900, p. 137, henceforth cited as Proceedings of Mo.

5. *Ibid*, p. 138.

6. Harold V. B. Voorhis, *Facts for Freemasons*, New York, Macoy, 1951, p. 201.

7. Proceedings of Mo., p. 138.

8. *Ibid*, p. 138.

9. Procedings of the Grand Lodge of Kentucky, 1898, p. 7.

10. Proceedings of Mo., p. 140.

11. *Ibid*, p. 140.

12. *Ibid*, p. 118.

13. *Negro Masonry in America*, a paper by Marshall E. Gordon, issued by Walter F. Meirer Lodge of Research No. 281, F. & A.M., Seattle, Washington, Approved for publication September 1964, p. 267.

14. Proceedings of the Prince Hall Grand Lodge of New York, 1920.

15. *A Masonic Digest for Freemasons in the Prince Hall Fraternity* by Harry A. Williamson, 1951, page 118, item No. 572 (Author's collection). In another paper, "The Names of Some Prince Hall Lodges," Bro. Williamson writes: The proceedings of the Prince Hall Grand Lodge of New York for

1918/1919, pages 160/161, carry a memorial to Upton. Pages 169/170 contain an account of how my Grand Lodge (of New York) had the graves of Upton, his wife and son, covered with flowers in connection with [the] Diamond Jubilee of my Grand Lodge. In a telegram received from Ernest H. Holmes, Grand Master of the Prince Hall Grand Lodge of Washington, he stated his eulogy was "Upton, The Brethren of New York have not forgotten you."

16. "The Names of Some Prince Hall Lodges" by Harry A. Williamson, (Authors Collection) page 6.

17. Prince Hall Yearbook, 1975, page 89.

18. The plaque was received by Past Grand Master J. William J. Stedman, Committee on Fraternal Correspondence on behalf of the Caucasian Grand Lodge of Washington.

REFERENCE FOR PART III

1. Caucasian Prince Hall Lodge appeared as an article in *The Philalethes Magazine* (Vol. XXX, April 1977. Number 2, p. 15) and, in turn, brought forth a response from Daniel M. Semel, D.D.G.M., Past Master and Historian of Shakespeare Lodge No. 750 F. & A.M., which added significant details to this interesting chapter in American Freemasonry. Semel's article appears in *The Philalethes Magazine*, Vol. XXXI, April 1978, Number 2, pp. 10-11.

X

PHYLAXIS—A SOCIETY IS BORN

In November 1787, in Philadelphia, Bro. Absalom Jones and Bro. Richard Allen were pulled from the knees while at worship and prayer at the Caucasian St. George Methodist Episcopal Church. Absalom Jones was the first Worshipful Master of the Second African Lodge No. 459 in Philadelphia; Richard Allen, its Treasurer. Prince Hall installed both in office. Absalom Jones became the first Prince Hall Grand Master of Pennsylvania, and the founder of the first Episcopal Church for Blacks in America. Richard Allen became the founder and first Bishop of the African Methodist Episcopal Church in America. The story of these two apostles of freedom is ably told by another Prince Hall Freemason, Bro. Charles H. Wesley, in his book by that name. (1) This may be a strange beginning to relate the history of the Phylaxis Society, yet there is a lesson to be seen.

Because of the combination of racism and bigotry these brethren of the Craft withdrew from the White church and created an independent church of their own. So often in the life of the Black man in America has he had to create his own institutions from which to gather strength! It is of little surprise that there is a parallel between this incident and the history of the Phylaxis Society.

The birth of the Society was a natural outcome of a social situation and its concept was nurtured as an idea whose time had come.

In the early 1970's a small number of editors representing various Prince Hall Masonic Jurisdictions began the interchange of their respective Grand Lodge official organs. Those involved were the editors of *The Light* from Pennsylvania, *The Masonic Quarterly* from Texas, *The Plumb Line* from Louisiana, *The Prince Hall Sentinel* from New York, *The Lamp* from Ohio, and *The Masonic Light* from Missouri.

The exchanging of these various publications was done in the hope that a strong bond, union and dialogue would develop, thereby creating more Masonic light, knowledge and information for the whole group. Towards this end, the Missouri *Masonic Light* printed a unique back cover as a salute to its counterparts under the banner "Let us join together to better serve our/individual Grand Lodge Jurisdictions."

From this seed was born the idea of the formation of some type of an organization of Prince Hall editors. The basic idea was later broadened to include Grand Lodge historians and Masonic writers as well, but no actual steps were taken to formalize such a body. It was, at that time and place, a mere play of words on paper.

During the same period, this writer, then editor of *The Masonic Light* of Missouri, began subscribing to a number of well-known Caucasian Masonic publications. The purpose was innocent enough, for there was a thirst for Masonic knowledge.

The publication that had the most profound and lasting effect was *The Philalethes* magazine, published by a remarkable Masonic research society of that name. Truly, it can be said, that this organization changed the Masonic life of this writer, and it eventually gave birth to a similar organization of Prince Hall Freemasons. Unfortunately, the new society did not emerge without some bitter words.

Through some strange twist of fate, this writer received an application for membership from the Executive Secretary of the Philalethes Society and, with a smile, filled it out and submitted it with the required fee. Within a short time a membership card was received and this Prince Hall Freemason joined a handful of other Prince Hall Masons who maintained membership "secretly" in the elite research group.

As could be expected, the Caucasian Society did not apply itself to Prince Hall Freemasonry in any respect, limiting its research only to its own racial group and fraternity. (2) After months of frustration, not only as a member of the Philalethes Society, but also with the inability of the Prince Hall editors to form into a group, the writer began to consider the feasibility of forming a like research society within the Prince Hall family.

With considerable thought as to quality and dedication to the Prince Hall fraternity as well as with the courage and strength to set out on a new path towards Masonic light, this writer made contact with fellow brethren of the Craft who had several things in common.

They had served together in the United States Army and had worked in King Solomon Lodge No. 15 F. & A.M. at Fort Leonard Wood, Missouri. Each also had a true love of the fraternity. Communication by telephone and through the mail system was established, and a formal Prince Hall Masonic research society was organized in 1973.

The name of these courageous brethren will be recorded in the pages of Prince Hall Masonic history. The fraternity owes to them its enduring gratitude. Bro. Herbert Dailey, retired from the military and residing in Tacoma, Washington, became the First Vice President; Bro. Zellus Bailey of St. Louis, Missouri, on active military status, became the Second Vice President; Bro. James E. Herndon, retired military residing in Denver, Colorado, became Executive Secretary; and Bro. Alonzo D. Foote, Sr., retired military also residing in Tacoma, Washington, became the Treasurer. Like this writer, all had careers in the U.S. Army.

The Greek word, Phylaxis, which means to safeguard and preserve, was adopted as its formal name. Its credo, like its Caucasian counterpart, became "A Society of Prince Hall Freemasons who seek more light, and who have light to impart." Its emblem became a Square and Compass resting on an open volume of sacred laws and over the lamp of knowledge, with the number "15" in its center. The "15" represents Prince Hall and the "14 Fellows of Color" raised with him. It was felt that, with this symbol, the Society would express its dual character of dedication to its founder Prince Hall and to the entire fraternity which bore that name.

In the meantime, in Boston, Massachusetts, a very unusual event occurred. A non-Mason, a "profane," published a pamphlet, titled *Negro Masonry in the United States*. This was the work of Arthur H. Frederick, who later became a member of the Prince Hall family and took his place within the newly-formed Society as its editor. He had the distinction of being the first "civilian" staff member.

As could be expected it wasn't long before the Philalethes Society got wind of the events taking place. They reacted by returning the joining fee to this writer, together with the following letter:

> "Your apparent membership in our Society was discussed at a meeting of the Executive Committee held in Washington, D.C., recently and we wish to advise you of the matter.
>
> "Section 2 of our By-Laws provides 'Members shall be Master Masons in good standing under a Grand Lodge of the United States. The qualifications of other applicants shall be decided by the Executive Committee.' It would appear that

you do not qualify for membership as you are not a Master Mason in good standing under a Grand Lodge of the United States. Your Lodge does not appear in the list of recognized Lodges in the United States. The member who signed your application for membership was not aware of this and the Secretary who processed the application did not consult the list of recognized Lodges in the United States. As a consequence, your membership was void from the start.

"This does not mean that you cannot be connected with the Society because Section 4 of our By-laws provides: 'Masonic bodies and individuals, not eligible to become Members of the Society, or who wish to receive the Philalethes Magazine, may become Subscribers.' You are therefore being classified as a Subscriber instead of a Member. We wish to emphasize that this action is not intended to cast any reflection on you as a person, but is merely a matter of internal classification under our by-laws.

"Accordingly, our records have been changed, and you are hereby notified that you are now classified as a Subscriber and not as a Member of our Society. We are sorry that this mistake came about, and we trust that you understand the position of the Executive Committee and will accept this change of classification in the same friendly spirit in which we approached this matter and resolved it. Your remittance for the joining fee is hereby refunded.

Yours very truly,
/s/ William E. Yeager, President"

In due time a second letter arrived, which was answered in part:

"September 1, 1974

"Dear Sir:

I have decided to break my silence, and to answer the March 4th letter from your late President, William E. Yeager, and the recent letter from Ronald E. Heaton, Treasurer, dated August 21st, concerning my membership in the Philalethes Society and the refunding of my joining fee.

"Needless to say I am quite bitter over the entire affair, and I reject and refuse to accept the return of my joining fee.

"Mr. Yeager, in his letter to me, quoted Section 2 of our By-Laws, i.e., Members shall be Master Masons in good standing under a Grand Lodge of the United States. The qualifications of other applications shall be decided by the Executive Committee. Here is where we go to court. I am a Master Mason in good standing under a Grand Lodge (Prince Hall) of the United States.

"In the words of W. G. Sibley, *The Story of Freemasonry* (1904, p. 72) Race prejudice exists to some extent among Freemasons, although properly it can have no place in so cosmopolitan an institution.... Racism obviously exists in the Philalethes Society."

During the same period in 1974, after a year of tip-toe planning, the Society launched its official entry into the Masonic research community, with its magazine *The Phylaxis*. It was a small effort of just

twelve pages, but a giant stride forward for Black Masonic frater-
nalism in the United States. (3)

The magazine began its global distribution throughout the United
States, Canada, and a number of U.S. Military bases overseas, and it
eventually found its way outside of its Prince Hall realm of influence,
being received in England, Germany and France. In Europe it came
as a pleasant surprise to the "old world" brethren who received and
welcomed the new entry into the Masonic research community. For
most Caucasians, Americans and Europeans, gaining access to the
Phylaxis magazine, was their first introduction to a world they knew
little of.

Acceptance of the Society by its own fraternity was not necessarily
that of open arms. There was some element of suspicion, skepticism
and cynicism as well as a degree of misconception by a few Grand
Masters. Some, without any investigation or inquiry, declared the
Society as an intrusion into their jurisdictions. Others felt they should
exercise control over the activities of the Society within their State,
and still others were downright hostile, going so far as to declare the
Society clandestine.

Some Grand Masters gave the impression that they felt threatened,
while a few expressed the belief that there was no need for a research
organization. They also expressed fears that the Society would expose
the "secrets" of the order, and they believed it was an innovation in
direct conflict with their conception of the landmarks of Masonry. At
the extreme point of controversy, rumors were spread that the Society
was printing a ritual.

Hostilities from quarters outside of the Prince Hall fraternity were
also received. Charges of discrimination in reverse were leveled by a
handful of Caucasians who sought membership and were gently turned down, not because of their race as they complained, but merely
because they were not Prince Hall Freemasons. This rejection in turn
angered some members within the Prince Hall fraterntiy.

Stranger still, other organizations, similar in concept, but outside
the pale of either "regular" or Prince Hall Freemasonry, decided
either that they should run the Society or that the Society should
follow their influence. Some went so far as to express annoyance over
the Society's use of the M.P.S., and suggested adoption of P.S.M. or
M.P.X. instead.

But while the Society had its share of detractors, it also picked up
many supporters within and without the Prince Hall Masonic family.

Surprisingly, a large number of members from the Philalethes Society applauded the efforts of the new organizaiton, and some submitted manuscripts for publication in the new magazine. They were first accepted as "guest writers," but the term was later dropped. Those, like Voorhis and Marsengill, were recognized throughout the Masonic community as being the foremost Masonic writers of their time.

The first member to be named a Fellow of the Society, also, had the rare distinction of receiving the Certificate of Literature Award as well. This dual honor was conferred upon Bro. Ira S. Holder, Sr., Grand Historian Emeritus of the Prince Hall Grand Lodge of New York. Both awards carried the date of March 6, 1975, the 200th Anniversary of the initiation of Prince Hall and 14 Blacks into the mystic tie. A significant honor for the deserving Brother. The Society issued the following statement at the presentation ceremonies:

> The Society honors a Prince Hall Masonic Scholar and historian, whose lectures appear in each issue of our Phylaxis Magazine, under title of "The Masonic Address and Writings of Ira S. Holder, Sr.," and his recent 'Masterpiece' "Stormy is the Road," which appears in our December ('75) issue, will be received enthusiastically throughout Masonic circles around the globe, in Masonic Libraries and Museums, but more especially to the members of the Prince Hall fraternity.
>
> Mankind has always experienced great difficulty in promoting great ideas and ideals through institutions of its own creation, such as the Phylaxis Society. Always the tendency has been work for the institution itself rather than the idea that gave it birth, and the ideals it fosters. This is true of the institution of Freemasonry.
>
> But then comes along one, like the honoree who has dedicated himself to the history, literature and lectures of Prince Hall Masonry in keeping with the goals and ideals of this research society.
>
> So it is only fitting that this Society of Prince Hall Freemasons, who seek more light and who have light to impart, to take time to honor Ira S. Holder, Sr. a Fellow of the Phylaxis Society.

Bro. Holder was an original advocate and supporter of the concept of the Society, and later one of its strongest backers. His Masterpiece completed for acceptance of the Fellow of the Society award was the hard hitting "Stormy is the Road." The Certificate of Literature was awarded for "The Complete History of Widow Son's Lodge No. 11 F. & A.M., Brooklyn, New York," a pamphlet co-authored with Courtenay L. Wiltshire, also a member of the Society.

While these positive results were being made, the Society quickly found itself involved in another controversy. A conflict which actually began prior to the Society publishing its first issue of its magazine. An event unfolded that would have wide implications and repercussions and after effects which would strain the Society's relations with the Prince Hall Grand Lodge of Michigan; and introduce it to the Universal League of Freemasons and its often brilliant, often paranoid Secretary, Harvey Newton Brown.

This writer, then editor of the Missouri *Masonic Light* reviewed two pamphlets, "*Symbolic Freemasonry Among the Negroes of America: An Answer to their Claims of Regularity and Legitimacy,*" by Thomas J. Harkins (4) and "*Freemasonry Among Negroes and Whites in America: A Study in Masonic Legitimacy and Regularity,*" by Harvey Newton Brown. (5) Brown's book was a masterful reply to Harkins' attack on Prince Hall Freemasonry, and the review praised Brown, and as a courtesy, sent him a copy of the *Masonic Light* to his home in El Paso, Texas.

From this began one of the strangest and bizarre periods for this writer and the new Society. In response to the courtesy copy of the magazine which lauded his work, Brown, a retired Army Lieutenant Colonel, forwarded a package of literature together with a letter, which contained several insulting statements to the fact that the Prince Hall Grand Lodge of Missouri was composed of "nothing but Uncle Toms!"

In response to this unprovoked affront, a letter was sent to the Caucasian Grand Lodge of Rhode Island, as Brown held membership there. The letter read in part:

"The Most Worshipful Prince Hall Grand Lodge F. & A.M. of Missouri and its Masonic Jurisdiction, its official organ, the *Masonic Light*, its Editor and Director of Public Relations and Prince Hall Masonry in general, has recently come under attack by a member of your Grand Lodge, LTC (R) Harvey N. Brown.

"The Most Worshipful Prince Hall Grand Lodge F. & A.M. is a sovereign Grand Lodge of Prince Hall Freemasons, conducting its own affairs, under its own Constitutions and By-Laws, within its own Masonic Jurisdiction. What right does the Caucasian Grand Lodge of Rhode Island to call us "Uncle Toms?"

"This direct racist attack by your Grand Lodge on the Grand Lodge of Missouri (PHA) will be dealt with in like manner." (6)

A reply was received:

"...anyone including ourselves, would regret the actions of Harvey N. Brown, who has run afoul of many Caucasian Grand Lodges. Mr. Brown does not speak for the Grand Lodge of Rhode Island and only one person can speak for it, and that is our Most Worshipful Grand Master.

"...I trust that in a moment of reflection, you will understand that actions of people along the lines which you described in your letter are not condoned or tolerated by our Grand Lodge.

Fraternally yours,

Albert W. Abramson, P.G.M.

Grand Secretary."

The first issue of the *Phylaxis Magazine* was published in January 1974, and with it, its first editorial, *"The U.L.F. and the Phylaxis Society"* which read:

"It is the official position of the Phylaxis Society as stated in our Newsletter, that the Universal League of Freemasons is 'Non-conducive' to Prince Hall Masonry. History has clearly showed us our mistakes in forming the National Grand Lodge or Compact, and it has cost us dearly, as this disbanded body invades our jurisdictions with their clandestine lodges.

"It has come to our attention that past Grand Master from the Most Worshipful Prince Hall Grand Lodge of Michigan has been appointed as National Deputy of the U.L.F. replacing a Deputy who was forced to withdraw his membership by the Grand Master of California.

"We cannot understand, why this P.G.M. would accept such a position, nor why he would join an organization that has been judged by American Masonic bodies, as Clandestine. The Phylaxis Society will not brand this organization as such, but we maintain that it is non-conducive to Prince Hall Masonry. The U.L.F. has shown by its newsletter to have an understanding attitude towards Prince Hall Masonry, and it has defended P.H.A. against racially motivated attacks from Caucasian Masonic bodies, but, the mere fact that it accepts 'regular, irregular and clandestine Masons' into its ranks is cause for the Phylaxis Society to take the stand that it does." (7)

There began a period in which abusive letters were exchanged, all being a far cry of the spirit of Freemasonry. Members began to complain of receiving applications for membership in the U.L.F., which forced the Society to stop publishing the complete address of its new members in the Welcome section of the *Phylaxis*, as this was being used as the basis of the U.L.F. mailing list. Various other "irritations" were being reported.

This entire period in the history of the young Society may rightfully be considered one of its lowest ebbs. It will be for those unbiased researchers of Masonic history to put the pieces of the jigsaw together and to pass their judgment over the entire affair.

The first annual Executive Meeting of the Society was held in Denver, Colorado, September 6-7, 1975. Among the many problem areas debated, was what to do with several Caucasian Freemasons who had involved themselves into the affairs of the Society. The Secretary of the Universal League of Freemasons had not only demanded membership in the Society but a number of his acts were judged to be quite detrimental, with an eye of not only discrediting the President, but an overt attempt to drive a wedge between the leadership of the Society.

The second was a former President of the Philalethes Society whose bitter views of the Society was discussed and dismissed as those either of a bigot or a very misguided individual. On the other hand, there were two Caucasian Freemasons from Iowa who had extended to the Society a hand of fraternal fellowship, had encouraged the new organization, and were accepted by it as fraternal friends.

The Society which had patterned itself after the Philalethes Society did not want a Masonic sham, that is, exclusiveness of membership based on race. It was agreed that Prince Hall Freemasonry accepted all men found worthy, race playing no part. That the fraternity was indeed made up of all races, therefore the Society by limiting its membership to Prince Hall Freemasons was not restricting membership to race. At the second annual Executive Session held in Seattle, Washington, March 5-6, 1976, the Society named two Caucasian Freemasons from Iowa, Bro. Keith Arrington and Bro. Jerry Marsengill, Honorary Fellows of the Phylaxis Society.

Gradual acceptance by the leadership of Prince Hall Freemasonry became evident when the Grand Master of Louisiana, John G. Lewis, Jr., the "dean" of Grand Masters (8), who wore a second hat as the Sovereign Grand Commander of the Ancient and Accepted Scottish Rite of Freemasonry, Southern Jurisdiction, himself a member, threw his support behind the young Society. At the 1975 annual Conference of Prince Hall Grand Masters meeting in Portland, Oregon, Grand Master Lewis in his presentation to the Conference supported the organization and its publication, explaining that "...it was the only document which crossed all jurisdictional lines." (9)

As an added inducement, the Conference printed the Society's complete four-page application for membership in its proceedings (10) and several Grand Lodges followed suit by recording worthwhile comments relative to the Society and its programs. (11)

The following year an invitation was extended to the President of the Society by Grand Master Lewis, to attend the 1976 Conference of Prince Hall Grand Masters meeting in Colorado Springs, Colorado.

> "I certainly would like to have your name placed on the agenda if such is possible, to have you speak about the promotion of the Phylaxis (Magazine). It is the best publication for Prince Hall Masonry that has appeared on the scene in a long time." (12)

While this event was unfolding, informational articles concerning the Society began appearing in a number of Masonic jurisdictional publications across the country and more Grand Masters were becoming members. Some were bringing their entire adminstrative staff into membership, while notifying their total jurisdiction of the Society and its goals.

The *Phylaxis Magazine* was finding its way to areas far and wide, while the Society began establishing communications that extended across the country and abroad as well.

The Society held its third annual Executive Session in March 1977, at Leavenworth, Kansas. Bro. Paul V. Best of Des Moines, Iowa, was elected to the office of Executive Secretary; Arthur H. Frederick became Second Vice President and Raymond T. Coleman became Editor of the *Phylaxis Magazine.* Frederick and Coleman were both from Roxbury, Massachusetts.

At this session, the First Vice President, Herbert Dailey, one of the three remaining Charter Members and Grand Master John G. Lewis, Jr., were recommended and approved as Fellows of the Society. Dr. Charles H. Wesley, author, historian and Masonic scholar named Fellow in 1976, was presented the Society's Certificate of Literature for his book, *Prince Hall: Life and Legacy.*

The Society continued its upward progress, as more and more Prince Hall Freemasons became members but it wasn't long before it found itself again involved in another controversy; this time a serious disagreement had arisen.

In 1978, the Society published two unique articles: "Fraternal Recognition" by John G. Lewis, Jr., Grand Master of Louisiana, and "The Power and the Glory," An In-depth Analysis of Prince Hall Freemasonry," by the Executive Secretary, Paul V. Best. Bro. Best's article, in reality a thesis, symbolically denoted in the organization's terminology as a "Masterpiece," which was submitted as part of the requirement for eligibility to become a "Fellow" of the Society. However, the two articles angered one Grand Master who was a member of the Society and set the stage again for a confrontation between the Society and the fraternity it was organized to serve.

The offended Grand Master found the following lines, written by Grand Master Lewis objectionable:

> "Another concern in which the roots of dissention are found is that of the legislation pertaining to female bodies to the effect that a female must join the Order of the Eastern Star before joining any of the other female orders.
>
> "There is no progression or succession in the female orders. Their membership is not predicated each upon the other. This is also true of their ritualistic work. Each is entirely independent and without reference to the other.
>
> "There can be found no responsible authority which equates the Order of the Eastern Star with the Symbolic Lodge. The Order of the Eastern Star is adopted by a Grand Lodge as an auxillary and not a counterpart or equal. The same is true of the other female bodies.
>
> "Each may be adopted as auxilliaries to the recognized and affiliated bodies. Certainly a Grand Lodge can pass such a regulation in the sense that it can and will do anything else it wishes, but such a regulation does not have the sanction of law or custom and its enactment is the assertion of an arbitrary will." (13)

The Grand Master also found several portions of Bro. Best's thesis equally offensive.

> "I have gone on the underlying belief and assumption that there is a distinct relationship between the decline of Prince Hall Grand Lodges and the tenure of the office of the Grand Master. Some Grand Lodges may have actually stunted the progress of their Grand Lodges without fully being aware of it..." (14)

As the conflict developed, the Society attempted to maintain a low profile, explaining that the views expressed by others, were not necessarily those of the organization. By presenting varying opinions, the Society argued, it gave to its members and readers a cross-section of differing viewpoints, allowing for acceptance or disapproval by readers as a personal choice. Exposure, at any rate, stimulates Masonic education.

On the other hand, the antagonized Grand Master was of the opinion that as the *Phylaxis Magazine* was an international publication, crossing all Masonic boundaries and jurisdictions, it had an obligation to expurgate views that would be considered offensive or objectionable to some Masonic jurisdictions.

As an illustration, he pointed out that his Grand Lodge had passed a requirement that all female members would have to come through the Order of the Eastern Star before "advancing" through the other adoptive female orders. Therefore a publication advocating other than that would be in direct disagreement with the edicts of that Grand Lodge.

Furthermore, his Grand Lodge maintained the system of tenureship and yet his Grand Lodge was progressive he believed.

The Society maintained its right to be free from censorship, declaring that otherwise it would not be in the best interests of Masonry, be un-Masonic and un-American as well. The article written by Grand Master Lewis had originally been published in the Proceedings of the Conference of Prince Hall Grand Masters, and the Society suggested that the Grand Master take his complaint to that body, it being a body of equals; and that the Society was designed to create a bond of union for Prince Hall Masonic writers and also to protect them from undeserved aggression by those "dressed in a little brief authority." (15)

It would maintain its integrity to publish articles felt to be in the best interests of its members and Prince Hall Freemasonry.

In an effort to find a solution, the Society offered space in its magazine to the Grand Master for rebuttal, which was accepted and published.

The controversy died as suddenly as it had begun and, ironically, the Grand Master would be forced by tenureship to step aside, refusing also to renew his membership in the Society.

Another area of concern, was the Caucasian Freemasons who had befriended the Society. Bro. L. Sherman Brooks, a Masonic calligrapher from Jamestown, New York, became the third "Honorary Fellow of the Society." What concerned the Society would be not knowing what reactions the Caucasian Grand Lodges would take in the naming of their members as Honorary members of the Society. The Society considered them progressive Freemasons in the spirit of William H. Upton and Joseph G. Findel and above the racism and pettiness of their individual Grand Lodges. The Society decided to continue to stretch forth its fraternal hand in friendship, but would avoid anything of a formal Masonic nature, thereby keeping the Honorary Members from conflicting with the dictates of their Grand Lodges.

The year 1978 began with an extraordinary sentimental and emotional journey for the Society. Its annual convention was in Boston, the Commonwealth of "The Master" Prince Hall.

The Society was invited by the Prince Hall Grand Lodge of Massachusetts and its Grand Master, a member of the Society.

For the members in attendance, representing the Society that was dedicated to the memory of Prince Hall and Prince Hall Freemasonry, it would be a most profound and unforgetable experience. What transpired, is recorded by the Executive Secretary:

> The breakfast adjourned with all members reassembling shortly for the excursion to the Boston Safe Deposit and Trust. For us this journey was an unparalleled experience. Not only had we made a pilgrimage to the Motherland from whence our seeds sprouted and our roots were firmly entrenched, we were to be granted a greater experience: of actually viewing and beholding the Historic Charter and other documents which have been sacred to Prince Hall Masons for more than 192 years. The same document which created so much controversy that even the U.S. Supreme Court rendered a decision of legitimacy. The actual number of people who have viewed these historic documents only number in the hundreds out of better than 300,000 Prince Hall Masons. Additionally, we were only the third organization to be granted permission from the M.W. Prince Hall Grand Lodge of Mass., to do so, save at the grand occasion every 10 years. (16)

> Words are somewhat inadequate to express our appreciation to M.W. Andrew J. Spears, Grand Master of Mass., and his cabinet for making this event possible. Because of his exemplification of brotherhood, we have been enshrined with an experience which marks the highest pinnacle of Masonic exposure to which a Prince Hall Mason can aspire. For this we are grateful and blessed.

> When the wooden vault was rolled out of the steel safe and into the security room in which we were assembled, and the seal broken, the silence was of such magnitude that even a pin falling onto the carpet would have resounded as a clap of thunder! The solemnity of this occasion marked an experience which shall be unequalled the remainder of our lives.

> The cherished documents are quite secure, legible and have been well cared for. While a complete listing of the inventory is not possible, we witnesed the Historic Charter (charred, because of a fire in 1869 but encased between two sheets of glass) Prince Hall's Letter Book, Prince Hall's Gavel, a gavel supposedly carved from an old auction block on slave row in Virginia, a Masonic medallion some 28 years old bearing a likeness of Prince Hall, and several other relics and items of general interest. Just to be able to touch...to hold in our hands these veritable artifacts left indescribable feelings. After extensively perusing and enjoying the occasion, the items were replaced in the chest and safely returned to the vault from whence they were hailed. The members formed an 'eternal chain' and paid homage to The Deity for having fulfilled our Masonic dream...an ecstatic and electrifying revelation. (17)

And so, this young Society was acquainting the Masonic community with the 200 year Prince Hall fraternity and in the process establishing itself as worthy of the cause it espoused. As it explained its views and opinions, attacking Masonic racism, ignorance and untruths concerning the Prince Hall solidarity, individualistic in its style, choosing its own paths, allowing none to dictate to it, but honestly working under the framework of its Charter for the betterment not only of Prince Hall Freemasonry, but the entire concept of Universal Freemasonry, its voice, sometimes brash and militant, was being heard.

What role it will play in the future is not known, of course. But that it shall play a role, is certain.

the phylaxis society ▽ the phylaxis society

The Phylaxis Society

awards the

Certificate of Literature

FOR 1977 to

BROTHER

Charles H. Wesley, F.P.S.

for his contribution to

the Literature of

prince hall masonry

on this 6th day of march 1977

15

chairman of fellows

president

E. Sherman Brooks

the phylaxis society ∨ the phylaxis society

The Phylaxis Society

in recognition of his
service to the society,
humanity and to
prince hall free masonry

most∴ worshipful∴ brother

John G. Lewis, Jr. M.P.S.

has been elected a

Fellow

of this society
on this 6th day of march 1977

chairman of fellows   president

C. Sherman Brooks

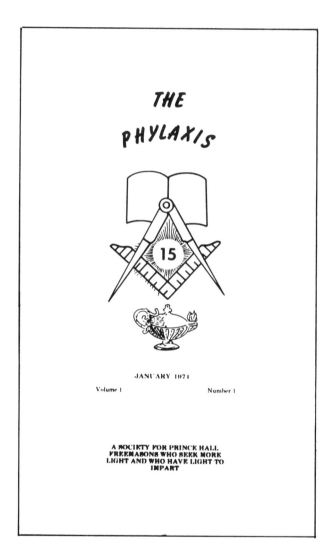

THE

PHYLAXIS

JANUARY 1974

Volume 1   Number 1

A SOCIETY FOR PRINCE HALL
FREEMASONS WHO SEEK MORE
LIGHT AND WHO HAVE LIGHT TO
IMPART

Cover of the first issue of The Phylaxis Magazine, January 1974

John G. Lewis, Jr., 33⁰

Dr. Charles H. Wesley, 33⁰

REFERENCES FOR PART X

1. Charles H. Wesley, *Richard Allen: Apostle of Freedom*, Washington, DC, The Associated Publishers, Inc., 1935.
2. Application was sent by Franklin J. "Andy" Anderson, then Executive Secretary.
3. The first issue was January, 1974.
4. Thomas J. Harkins, P.G.M., *Symbolic Freemasonry Among Negroes of America: An Answer to their Claims of Legitimacy and Regularity*, Asheville, North Carolina, Foreword by Luther A. Smith, 33⁰, Sovereign Grand Commander, Southern Jurisdiction, U.S.A.
5. Harvey Newton Brown, *Freemasonry Among Negroes and Whites: A Study in Masonic Legitimacy and Regularity* (privately published).
6. Letter dated May 11, 1974 to Albert W. Abramson, PGM.
7. *Phylaxis*, January 1974, p. 4.
8. Grand Master Lewis succeeded his brother, Scott A. Lewis as Grand Master of Louisiana in 1941. He was elected Sovereign Grand Commander of the United Supreme Council, A.A.S.R., Southern Jurisdiction in October 1961, remaining in both offices, until his death in 1979.
9. Proceedings of the 58th Session, Conference of Prince Hall Grand Masters, May 7-9, 1975, pp. 35-40.
10. *Ibid*, pp. 51-53.
11. Proceedings, Prince Hall Grand Lodge of Louisiana, June 17-19, 1975, p. 82; Proceedings, Prince Hall Grand Lodge of Texas, June 17-29, 1978, p. 33; Proceedings, Prince Hall Grand Lodge of Iowa, July 8, 1976, p. 59; Proceedings, Prince Hall Grand Lodge of Missouri, July 14-16, 1976, p. 26 and Missouri, July 12-14, 1978, p. 65.
12. Letter from John G. Lewis, Jr., to Joseph A. Walkes, Jr. March 12, 1976.
13. *Phylaxis Magazine*, 4th Quarter, 1978, pp. 42-43.
14. *Phylaxis Magazine*, 3rd Quarter, 1978, p. 31.
15. Application for membership, Phylaxis Society which reads: "The Phylaxis Society was designed to create a bond of union from Prince Hall Masonic writers and also to protect editors of Masonic publications from undeserved aggression of some 'dressed in a little brief authority.' It might be easy to pick out an isolated individual, but the prospect of being held up to the scorn of the whole Prince Hall Fraternity outside one's own jurisdiction would give cause for pause."
16. The Conference of Prince Hall Grand Masters meeting in "pilgrimage" in Boston every ten years, visiting the monument to Prince Hall, at the grave site of his wife, Sarah Ritchery, in Copps Hill Burial Grounds. Contrary to popular belief, the actual burial site of Prince Hall is unknown. The markings on the tombstone "Here lies y Prince Hall" was

probably done prior to the celebration of the one hundreth anniversary of the granting of Charter 459 to Prince Hall.

17. Mission Accomplished! by Paul V. Best, Transactions, Phylaxis Society, March 3-5, 1978, pp. 1-2.

EPILOGUE

Several years ago there was a popular television series about New York City which ended each show with the statement, "there are eight million stories in the Naked City; this has been one of them!"

And so it is with the Prince Hall Masonic fraternity; its Lodges and Grand Lodges have countless interesting fruits on their respective historical trees, and they only await those who have the interest and the love, the dedication and the devotion, to bring them to light. This is what I have attempted to do.

While browsing through the various Grand Lodge proceedings, I have seen hints and suggestions of the role that the fraternity and individual Prince Hall Freemasons played in helping run-away slaves through the Underground Railroad and in avoiding the effects of the Fugitive Slave Act. They have been active in defending cities during epidemics; and in the reactions of the Craft to massive race riots, lynchings, and prejudiced court proceedings. And they have played an important role in the Black church, the education of children, the building of Black communities, the sustaining of a race, and the list is without end.

Throughout the wars fought by the United States, Masonic Lodges followed the troops, and after the hostilities (in some cases during hostilities), Prince Hall Military Lodges and Study Clubs sprung up wherever there was an American military presence. Their good deeds and acts were graciously beneficial to the foreign communities where the Lodges were located—Germany, France, Italy, England, Japan, Okinawa, Guam, Korea, Taiwan, The Philippines, Greece and a number of other countries.

In Korea, for instance, in 1970, when racial animosity had reached unbearable levels between Black GI's and Korean Nationals, the Commanding General of the United Nations Command/United States Forces Korea/Eighth United States Army had to reach to the Prince Hall Military Lodge in Seoul to help cool the situation. The Lodge initiated a concept dubbed by the Army as "GIT" (Get It Together), a program aimed at bringing peace between the Black Americans and Korean Nationals. As the Republic had a nationwide midnight to 6:00 A.M. curfew, with no one (Korean or American) allowed on the

165

streets during those hours, the Lodge began sponsoring all night dances at the famed "Chosen" Hotel in Seoul. American military personnel from throughout the Republic would attend the all-night festivities and tension between the Black military personnel and their Korean host eased.

Prince Hall military Lodges in Europe, more than twenty in number, played a major role in sustaining the American military community in the old world. Blacks as well as Caucasians flocked to Lodge, which played a most important social and moral role to thousands so far from home. Masonic leaders, such as George B. Swanson, would become a Masonic household name throughout the entire worldwide military community. These European Lodges reflected the military environment with strict dress codes, promptness in opening the Lodges, Masonic trials for offenses, fines for unauthorized absences, and a closeness and comraderie that marked their military training. Often these military Masons returning to the United States and affiliating with a Lodge composed of civilians would become the driving force behind the Lodge, demanding new programs, often impatient and critical of the slothfulness of their civilian counterparts. The finest example of the Lodges in Europe can be seen in its charitable contributions, often purchasing food and clothing for orphanages in the locality of the Lodges. In the Canal Zone money was raised by the Lodge members to help a young Panamanian girl to fly to the United States for open-heart surgery.

The most impressive gregarious occasions are to be seen in the Masonic social banquets and balls presented all over the world wherever there is an American military presence. The local nationalities are given a chance to see the well-mannered conduct of the Prince Hall Freemason at their social best.

Christmas is always a special and warm occasion. Prince Hall Freemasons around the globe, in the time-honored Masonic tradition of sharing and giving, have lifted the hearts of little children by the special yule-tide gatherings sponsored by the Lodges.

These brethren are not the "ugly Americans" that so many have been led to believe exist. On the contrary, for here are Prince Hall Freemasons practicing the "Royal Art" as did Prince Hall and the members of African Lodge 200 years prior.

Whatever is in store for the Masonic fraternity in America in the future and for those who will have to pass judgment on it, the role of the Prince Hall Freemason must be considered as one of the most glorious chapters in the pages of American history.

ADDENDA

THE MAKING OF A MASONIC BOOK

A Paper By
Joseph A. Walkes, Jr., F.P.S.
President, Phylaxis Society
Fifth Executive Session of The Phylaxis Society
Des Moines, Iowa, March 1979

With the completion of my book, whose title *Black Square & Compass: 200 Years of Prince Hall Freemasonry* was as elusive as the final printing of the book itself; many thoughts come to mind. I had kept a diary while writing the work and, as I read over the many notes, a vivid picture of the number of false starts, the many areas attempted to be covered, the many disappointments and the often frustrations come to mind. While I may paint a very negative and bleak picture, needless to say there were moments of satisfaction as well.

It would be somewhat redundant to detail each step of the process, so I will attempt to avoid this pitfall and concentrate on areas that might be helpful to others who may contemplate tackling such a project.

The question arises, why write a Masonic book? Certainly there is no financial profit to be derived in producing a book with such a restrictive reading audience. This can be seen by Harvey Newton Brown's book *Freemasonry among Negroes and Whites in America: A study in Masonic Legitimacy and Regularity* of which one thousand copies were printed privately by the author. Of this number, Brown ended up giving many copies away, in fact review copies were sent to each of the Prince Hall Grand Lodges and very little interest was shown.

Another example is Dr. Charles H. Wesley's efforts. Two thousand five hundred copies of his book *Prince Hall: Life and Legacy* were printed in 1977, which represents one percent or less of the total population of Prince Hall Freemasons. As of this date this supply has not been exhausted. So without doubt financial gain is not a factor, as Haki R. Madhubuti noted in the Nov/Dec issue of *The Black Scholar*, "...my observation is that I do not see book buying or borrowing high in the priority list of black people. To put it more emphatically, reading (or research and study) as a necessary life enrichment experience is not foremost in the *must do* list of most black people."

The writer of a Masonic work feels that he has something to add to the knowledge of the Craft, and it is important enough that he is willing to spend not only his time and energies, but his funds as well for what he considers beneficial to Freemasonry.

The work on the book began January 25, 1975. The title was then *Tales of Prince Hall Masonry*. Chapter One opens with the life of the founder of the fraternity that respectfully carries his name: Prince Hall. The idea was to present an up-to-date view of the life of the man the Phylaxis Society calls "The Master," and to clearly warn the reader of the Grimshaw fabrications and of the pitfalls of accepting Masonic history *per se* without verifying one's facts.

Unbeknown to me at the time, two other Masonic historians were researching the life of Prince Hall. One presented a definitive book on the subject not only to the Prince Hall Craft but to the entire Masonic community. The other presented a paper before the premier research lodge, the famed Quatuor Coronati Lodge 2076, London, England. Dr. Charles H. Wesley labored in the United States and his counterpart, George Draffen of Newington, in Scotland. Bro. Wesley would send me his completed manuscript to review before the final printing of his book, and I would also receive the galley proofs of Bro. Draffen's paper from a confidential source with the Grand Lodge of England, before it would become a part of the *Transactions* of that body.

Within both works I found areas to which I took exceptions, and communicated my feelings to each respective writer. Such is the nature of Masonic research—to raise questions; to raise objective exceptions, as the truth is often elusive. Masonic researchers should never relax in the pursuit of truth, as it is a duty always to press forward in the search for truth. Masonry itself is in a continual struggle toward the light.

I had decided to include in my research effort Prince Hall's two charges to African Lodge as well as his petition to the Senate and

House of Representatives of the Commonwealth of Massachusetts. I would later think better of that idea, and withhold them from the complete chapter, as they were included in Wesley's book. Of interest in my diary is the notation and reminder to myself, "not to be too critical of Caucasian Masonry!" Throughout my entire work this would cause me the most difficulties and concern. I admit that I was not successful in holding back criticism. Albert Pike wrote that "the truth comes to us tinged and colored with our prejudices and our preconceptions, which are as old as ourselves, and strong with a divine force." In order to be objective, the historian must keep a detached distance from his subject, keeping his personal feelings and views to himself. I found this to be an ever-constant struggle. As a Masonic historian, I am aware of the abuse that Prince Hall Freemasons have suffered at the hands of "regular" Freemasonry; it is difficult to bite one's tongue or remain silent on this subject.

By the next day I had completed 17 pages and had decided there were a number of areas that were weak and needed to be strengthened by adding various quotes from the works of other historians. Again, I would remind myself not to criticize Caucasian Freemasonry and added to the page of the diary "not to proclaim the regularity of Prince Hall Freemasonry. Not interested in proving anything, other than the fact that racism does appear in American Masonry!"

I had added to my ever-growing Masonic library a pamphlet, *Prince Hall the Pioneer of Negro Masonry*, written in 1921 by John Edward Bruce, better known under his journalist pen name of "Bruce Grit." This work arrived from the New York Public Library on the 29th of January. The author, a very famous newspaper man, curiously wrote that "Prince Hall was employed as a steward on one of the many vessels plying between Boston and England and that African Lodge had evolved from a little club in Boston." This statement by Bruce I found to be astonishing and included it in the chapter.

The first day of February would bring a letter from Bro. Ira S. Holder, Sr., Past Grand Historian from the Prince Hall Grand Lodge of New York, taking exception to the title of the book. He was adamantly against the word "tales" and suggested that "facts" be used in its stead.

No book is accomplished alone. It takes suggestions, ideas and criticisms from all parties that take an interest. These inputs motivate and keep the struggling writer on an even keel. Letters arrive and trigger various feelings. Some are objective and some emotional as my

169

diary notes that a letter was received from Harold V. B. Voorhis author of *Negro Masonry in the United States.* The diary records that "Voorhis withdrew his popular book from the market. He had based his work on the falsehood of William H. Grimshaw's so-called *Official History of Freemasonry among the Colored People of North America.* I note that Voorhis' book was selling for $20.00 at McBlain Book Store in Des Moines, Iowa, while Grimshaw's book sold for $16.50 in Plainview, New York. Both have long been out of print.

Later research by Edward Cusick of New York, John M. Sherman of Massachusetts, both anti-Prince Hall advocates, and others, brought forth new evidence proving without a doubt that Grimshaw had allowed his imagination to run wild, such as copying Henry Prince's Provincial Grand Master authorization, Prince Hall's alleged birth in the West Indies, his alledged service in the Continential Army, his allegation that Nero Prince, the Deputy Grand Master of the African Grand Lodge was Caucasian, and other fabrications. I asked myself how could Voorhis, a proven historian, have allowed himself to accept such assertions without verifying his facts. The truth of the matter as I saw it, was the fact that Voorhis had no dealings with the Black man, and therefore no knowledge of his history or his literature, and it would be there that he would have to go to write about the Black experience.

Grimshaw, a Past Grand Master from the Prince Hall Grand Lodge of Washington, D.C., certainly did a disservice to Prince Hall Masonry, a fact that is mentioned over and over in the first chapter of my book. The fact remains that Prince Hall was an outstanding individual. Considering the racism during that period in which he lived, he and his followers were remarkable. The fact that Cusick, Voorhis, Sherman and other Caucasians attempt to belittle the first Black Freemasons in America shows the sickness that is prevalent in American Freemasonry. Prince Hall Masonry is a fact of life and will remain so. The fact that Caucasian Masonry does not accept it, and has attacked it for 200 years, will always leave them open to the charge of racism. A charge that there is no defense against, because it is true. Racism will eventually destroy the American system of Masonry as we know it today, and what would happen if Prince Hall Freemasons began to picket Caucasian Masonic gatherings across the country calling attention to their anti-American, anti-Black, anti-Masonic stance. Part of this statement would find its way into the book.

Several days later, the same mood is carried as my diary records, "while reviewing the letter of Edward R. Cusick to John M. Sherman under the title of historical analysis, Cusick's questions and assertions seem logical at first light, yet the one area that he fails to consider is racism. This is the over-riding factor and alone negates his theories. Rev. Elliott's letter to Balknapp clearly shows the racism of the day when he notes, "that Whites and Blacks do not sit in Lodge together!"

By the 23rd of February, I destroyed all that had been written, and would begin anew. I decided to place the life of Prince Hall in chronological order, and completed ten pages in four hours. These new pages left me elated and feeling they were a vast improvement over the first version. All comments and references concerning racism or regularity were left out. Thus, I continued struggling with this emotional issue, and by the 19th of March there would be 26 pages completed with the end of the chapter in sight.

From that date for a period covering two months, nothing was accomplished as the book was set aside. When I resumed a new title was chosen, this being, *The Black Man: His Square and his Compass,* and the decision was made to include a catalogue of the items in my library as Chapter Ten. This idea would later be abandoned and Chapter Ten would carry the formation of the Phylaxis Society instead.

Work began on Chapter Two, "The Story of the Watch Chain," and nine days later it was completed with 22 pages to include references.

Chapter Three was begun. This was also to be a short chapter. I had decided to add the famous sermon of John Marrant to African Lodge. Of interest is the fact that this sermon may be the first printed document by a Black in the United States. Brief summaries on the life of Prince Saunders, Captain Paul Cuffee (the pre-Revolutionary War ship builder), James Forten of Philadelphia who, like Prince Hall, sent appeals to the Senate of Pennsylvania condemning slavery; Richard Allen and Absalom Jones, all extraordinary Prince Hall Freemasons of that era were added to give the chapter more balance.

By the first of June this chapter was increased by 21 pages together with a half page of references. The addition of the post-Revolutionary War period Masonic brethren gave considerable substance to the concept that the history of the Black man in America and the history of Prince Hall Freemasonry coincide.

Two weeks later Chapter Three consisting of 36 pages was completed and work was begun on my favorite section, Chapter Four, *Prince Hall Masonry and the Civil War*. This was indeed a glorious period in the Black struggle for freedom. A period when the race fought to lift the inhuman burden of slavery off its back. A period which is not fully recorded in the history books, and for the most part does not take note of the role of the Black man in fighting to free himself, or to preserve the Union from those who would destroy it by a rebellious insurrection in the name of slavery. That Prince Hall Freemasons were actively involved in combating this evil upholds the concept of the book, which is to show the relationship of Prince Hall Freemasonry to the Black experience in America. The discovery of one Prince Hall Military Lodge and verification of the other will remain to me the essence of the entire book.

The title of the book would continue to change, as I accepted new combinations of words, only to discard them until the title it presently carries hit the right tone to my way of thinking.

In conclusion, let me say that with this work goes the hope that a minute portion of the history of Prince Hall Freemasonry will be recorded; and that those who scorn the concept of the role of the Craft in the Black experience in America will better understand and appreciate the contributions made by it, as well as the role of Caucasian Freemasonry to hinder and destroy this institution. Therefore, if this book is accepted in this Light, then I have not failed in my task as a Masonic historian and will have made a small contribution to Freemasonry.

INDEX

174